"With the explosion of alerts, the once-lowly press release is now an incredibly effective way to reach your buyers directly. But this is not your father's press release. Janet Meiners Thaeler (Newspapergrl to her fans) will show you exactly how to harness the power of news releases to expand your business."
David Meerman Scott, bestselling author of 'The New Rules of Marketing & PR' and 'World Wide Rave'

"Don't write a press release for online distribution until you read this book. I love Janet Thaeler's easy-to-understand tips and illustrations on how to optimize your press releases for the search engines. Smart Publicity Hounds know that SEO, done correctly, will help Google find your releases, give them good ranking, and deliver them to people who are searching for the type of information you're writing about. This book should be must-reading for journalism students, PR pros, publicists, and anyone who writes their own releases."
Joan Stewart, The Publicity Hound
PublicityHound.com

"Wait! Before you issue your next press release, you must read PR Road Trip! Your press release, and your boss, will thank you!"
Andy Beal, coauthor of Radically Transparent
(http://www.andybeal.com)

"Janet's guide to Online PR is a comprehensive tutorial to writing, publishing, and marketing a Rank-5 PRWeb online press release. I'm amazed that Janet shared all her trade secrets. Get sample email pitches and learn to optimizing your Facebook and Twitter accounts. She writes step-by-step for anyone from an online newbie to a seasoned online pr expert. Grab these Insider Tips. I doubted I'd learn anything new but I learned a lot!"
Ponn M. Sabra, best-selling author, founder of American Muslim Mom online magazine AmericanMuslimMom.com

"When you finally understand the power of press, and what it does for branding, reputation, link building, traffic, and conversions for your business, it will be all you think about. Gaining links to your site via a press release is one of the most powerful forms of link building today. SEO is all about content and links. The more trust and authority you have, the more links. How do you get more trust and authority when you are brand new? You create it yourself, by getting the word out about yourself (via press of course). But it's not just for new websites. I have been marketing online businesses for over a decade, and marketing with press is still one of the main strategies I still use after all these years!"

Mat Siltala, SEO expert and owner of Dream Systems Media,
http://www.dreamsystemsmedia.com

I Need a Killer Press Release—Now What???

A Guide to Online PR

By Janet Meiners Thaeler
Foreword by Anita Campbell

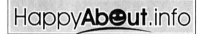

20660 Stevens Creek Blvd., Suite 210
Cupertino, CA 95014

Copyright © 2009 by Happy About®

First Printing: September 2009
Paperback ISBN: 978-1-60005-154-8 (1-60005-154-5)
Place of Publication: Silicon Valley, California, USA
Paperback Library of Congress Number: 2009935252

eBook ISBN: 978-1-60005-155-5 (1-60005-155-3)

Trademarks

Warning and Disclaimer

Acknowledgments

Thank You

The following people I have a lot of respect for and who influenced my understanding of online press releases:

Joe Beaulaurier and Mario Bonilla whom I met through PRWeb

Lee Odden

David Meerman Scott

There were also countless bloggers who inspired me, including my good friend Paul Wilson (http://www.mymarketer.net) who got me started on this journey. I'll never forget the day he was hired and told me about online marketing. I thought it was too good to be true, but it wasn't. Thank you for your contribution.

A Message from Happy About®

Thank you for your purchase of this Happy About book. It is available online at http://happyabout.info/killer-press-release.php or at other online and physical bookstores.

* Please contact us for quantity discounts at sales@happyabout.info
* If you want to be informed by email of upcoming Happy About® books, please email bookupdate@happyabout.info

Happy About is interested in you if you are an author who would like to submit a non-fiction book proposal or a corporation that would like to have a book written for you. Please contact us by email editorial@happyabout.info or phone (1-408-257-3000).

Other Happy About books available include:

* I'm on LinkedIn—Now What???:
  http://happyabout.info/linkedinhelp.php
* I'm on Facebook—Now What???:
  http://happyabout.info/facebook.php
* I've Got a Domain Name—Now What???:
  http://happyabout.info/ivegotadomainname.php
* I Need a Branded Bio—Now What???:
  http://happyabout.info/ineeda-brandedbio.php
* Marketing Thought: Tools and Strategies that Drive Results:
  http://happyabout.info/MarketingThought.php
* Twitter Means Business:
  http://happyabout.info/twitter/tweet2success.php
* 42 Rules for Driving Success With Books:
  http://42rules.com/driving_success_with_books/
* 42 Rules of Marketing:
  http://happyabout.info/42rules/marketing.php
* 42 Rules to Jumpstart Your Professional Success:
  http://happyabout.info/42rules/jumpstartprofessionalservices.php
* Happy About Online Networking:
  http://happyabout.info/onlinenetworking.php
* The Emergence of The Relationship Economy:
  http://happyabout.info/RelationshipEconomy.php
* Tales From The Networking Community:
  http://happyabout.info/networking-community.php
* Marketing Campaign Development:
  http://happyabout.info/marketingcampaigndevelopment.php

Contents

Contents

Foreword by Anita Campbell

One of the key small business trends we've been following over the past 5 years is the dramatic change in public relations. The web, and the rise of online press release tools, blogs, and social media websites, has flipped PR on its head.

PR now takes place in large part online.

And that's a great thing for small businesses.

Today, you can be in control of your own public relations. With online PR, you no longer have to work through others to get your story told. Now you can tell it directly—to the entire world. Your announcement or story can be picked up not just by journalists but also on blogs, through press release sites, and ultimately by search engines.

Online PR is just like it sounds: essentially you are publicizing your brand and products and services online. Tactics include submitting press releases to PR sites that syndicate them to various outlets. And with the rise in blogs (there are literally millions of them today), you can also quickly submit press releases to bloggers—as well as to traditional journalists.

Online PR also involves something I'm passion-ate about—social media: Twitter, Facebook, LinkedIn, and similar sites. Social media sites enable your news to spread even wider. Social media "amplifies" the messages that appear on other websites, and allows them to spread faster and to more people.

This opens up enormous opportunities for businesses of all sizes, but especially small businesses.

First of all, your costs can be kept low. Online PR is an ideal way to save money yet still proactively grow your business. During a recession, opportunity opens the door while your competitors are distracted. Take advantage of the opportunity through online PR, and not only will you be prepared when the slowdown ends, you'll be well-positioned to grow your business to the level you dream.

With online PR you also gain speed—and we all know how important speed to market is. Need a press announcement out within a couple of days? No problem. The web is available 24/7.

We've all read a book or watched a presentation that is long on theory but leaves you wondering where to start. It's easy to get overwhelmed by all the tasks you "need" to do to market a business. There is pressure to "do it all" and in the world of social media, that can mean spending a lot of time with little to show for it—unless you have a plan. That's why you need a practical guide.

When you don't have a lot of money to market, you have to come up with creative techniques. In 'I Need a Killer Press Release, Now What???' you will get past the theory and get straight to practical guidelines. You'll see precisely how to use tools like Twitter, PRWeb, HARO, Google Insights for Search, and social sites to increase your visibility and authority online.

I am very familiar with Janet Meiners Thaeler. I'm proud to call her one of the hand-picked contributors at my independent publication, Small Business Trends. Having read many articles by her, I know what she is good at. She's good at giving practical and solid advice, and painting a roadmap you can follow.

In this book you get the essential information you need to get publicity for your business, build brand awareness by the public, drive traffic to your website, and trigger positive word-of-mouth about your business. Put it all together with what small businesses are best at—creativity—and you have a winning formula for achieving your business goals.

Large companies spend millions every year in advertising and PR. The good news is a small business doesn't have to spend millions or go through a PR firm to get found online. Now you get equal footing with larger businesses—and even get *more* online visibility than some large businesses—while spending a fraction of what they spend.

Anita Campbell

This book is written for the small business owner who needs to learn how to use press releases and social networking sites to expand their marketing online. It's also for the PR pro who wants to master the Internet part of PR and offer online PR services to their clients.

I mention online news distributor PRWeb (http://www.PRWeb.com) often in the book because it is my most trusted source to distribute news online. PRWeb consistently ranked the highest in search engine rankings. I've always gotten excellent customer support and great results for myself and for my clients and, compared to traditional wire services, it's a good value.

By applying what you learn in this book, you'll see big improvements in your results for a fraction of what you'd pay for advertising—and it will have a much longer visibility span than advertising.

I'm going to tell you a secret—the press release, as a way to reach the media, is essentially dead. There are far better ways than sending out a press release to get traditional media coverage—most of that includes responding to inquiries and building relationships with journalists. Online you can get visibility through social media, your own blog and by using online distribution services to spread the news.

Where online press releases shine is in getting you noticed online in search engines where it's easier for people to find your news and therefore your business. It's very good for that. And many times the coverage you get online will take you much further than a great story in a newspaper or magazine. You can trace sales directly from a press release.

Some businesses I know have gotten coverage in major magazines or newspapers but say they get more sales and a larger response from getting online visibility. A write-up about your business in a popular blog like Entrepreneur.com can get you more mileage than being mentioned in a column in Newsweek. Getting your business on a blog or social media site might not have the glory and prestige associated with getting your name in print, but if it increases your ROI who's complaining?

Because the Internet is so dynamic, by the time you are reading this, some of the data will be outdated. There will be new tools, sites, and fads but the principles will remain. Marketing and communicating online is more about listening to, facilitating, measuring, and participating in conversations rather than controlling them. I'm providing tools to help you write, promote, and develop PR campaigns. You can then use social media, online press release distribution services (both free and paid) and your online networks to get the word out about your news.

The principles in this book will be relevant even if the tools change dramatically. This is not fast marketing like advertisements—it's building trust and helping others interact with your business. It takes time and consistency but can have large payoffs for your effort. People don't do business with companies, they do business with people. And to do business with people you must show a human side, one that others can relate to.

Remember, when it comes to online PR you CAN:

- Start a conversation

- Encourage others to start a conversation by giving key influencers something to talk about

- Publicize conversations

- Participate in conversations

- Monitor conversations

- Respond to people in conversations

But there's one thing you cannot do. That is, you cannot *control* the conversations. You have to give up control. It's not possible anyway. Approach online PR with this mindset. Give something to a community that they will value. These are the guiding principles of online PR.

I'm convinced that every business has amazing stories to tell but they are often overlooked. Look for and keep an eye out for those stories and then tell them. When something you do starts to catch on and create a small buzz or interest, use online PR tools to "fan the fire." These include blogs and social bookmarking and networking websites where you can share and promote your news. You can even use these tools to quickly learn about and respond to bad news.

Using the tips and techniques in this book, you'll soon be a press release and online PR ninja.

1 Online Press Releases Defined

Online press releases, social networking and blog are the foundation of online PR. What is the difference between a regular press release and an online press release? According to Answers.com a traditional press release is:

> An announcement of a newsworthy item that is issued to the press.

The purpose of a traditional press release is to get media coverage. It has a short shelf life of a few days. It's only seen by the media who usually get it via fax or email.

An online press release is a press release that is written for a variety of audiences on the Internet and distributed online. Online press releases have elements of traditional press releases but are often written less formally. They have a different style of writing. They include elements such as links, images, video, and SEO (or search engine optimization—which is a way of marketing so your website shows up high on the list of websites when someone types in words or phrases that relate to your business) factors.

An online press release is issued not just to the press but also to bloggers, customers, and to websites. It's written for many audiences including directly to a potential customer. Perhaps most importantly, an online press release is indexed by search engines where it becomes a permanent record about your business, where people can find and read it for years after its release.

My love for press releases as online marketing tools began when I worked at a small business as a technical marketer. The marketing department had one employee—me. I wanted to make a good impression on my new boss. I looked over the press releases from our PR firm. They had just one link to the corporate website.

I asked my boss if I could optimize and distribute our press releases online. I changed the sentences by adding keywords that linked to relevant pages of our website and submitted the press releases to PRWeb.

I didn't know much about the submission process then, but I still got results. PRWeb has various distribution packages at different prices. I experimented with different levels of payment to see which got the best results and published the results on my blog. Here are the numbers (impressions are the number of people who have seen the headline):

Week #1

PRWeb Payment Level	Impressions
$120 Press Release	over 18,000
$200 Press Release #1	over 70,000
$200 Press Release #2	just over 70,000

Now a *few days* later I could see the long tail of PRWeb press releases. Unlike traditional media that has a short shelf life online PR keeps growing because it has permanence online. There the number of people who see your news, click on it and download documents keeps increasing. I noticed that pickups (the number of places the news was reprinted or written about and prints (people who clicked on the link to print out a copy of the press release)continued to grow. If I logged into that same PRWeb account I started with today all of the numbers would be significantly higher. Even a week makes a difference as new people continue to find your news online.

PRWeb keeps your press release on their site indefinitely and people searching the Internet or their site continue to find it. You have a permanent URL and it continues to bring traffic to your website.

I'd rather pay once for traffic over time than have my press release accessible only for a few weeks. Those press releases I wrote years ago are still online today.

Week #2

PRWeb Payment Level	Impressions
$120 Press Release	over 35,000
$200 Press Release	over 78,000
$200 Press Release	over 70,500

Week #3

Payment Level	Impressions
$120 Press Release	over 39,000
$200 Press Release	over 84,000
$200 Press Release	just over 71,000

Here is the amazing part—for the next five months, after the news went out, PRWeb was one of the top five referrals to the site.

> That means a single press release distributed on PRWeb was responsible for most of the traffic to our website—for over five months.

I did this test several years ago and show it to you so you can get an idea of what to expect. I've worked on many press releases for businesses of all sizes and each is unique in the results. I watch the statistics and constantly learn, test, and apply to find out what works best. When people ask me if it's worth to pay $200 to distribute their news through PRWeb I suggest they test it like I did. Compare it against traditional wire services, different online news services, and free sites. Compare costs and results. Find what works best for your business. In online marketing and online PR you track and compare results to see what works best in your industry and see what distribution model works best for different types of news.

Tell a Story with Your News

When it comes to a press release, I love getting the story behind the news. The story is what makes news compelling. It's what news is all about. It's the human interest or the inside scoop that makes people care about your company. If you can tie your story into a larger story or current trend you have it made. *Why?* People love a good story. When it comes to a press release or media coverage, people usually don't care about your company unless you give them a reason to. A story gives them a reason. Your news is nothing without a story. Don't just tell us the news; make it interesting.

Your Audience has Expanded Online

With online press releases, you're not only speaking to reporters, but to the consumer directly and indirectly through search engines like Google. Reach the media with a pre-made story that is compelling enough to interest them in writing about it. Reach bloggers who may write about your story and link to it, helping it gain authority in search engines. Last, remember you're trying to find potential customer or clients and inspire them to take an action or get more visibility.

Rather than just being straight text, online press releases usually include links to websites and other elements crafted to get search engine traffic. An online press release can include these elements:

- Links to related web pages

- Images and other files embedded and/or attached to the press release

- Videos, PDF documents, audio files, or podcasts

- Social bookmarking tools like Delicious, Digg, or StumbledUpon

- RSS feeds—essentially a subscription model so people can easily get updates and know when there is new information released.

Strategic linking and a logo or picture of a product highlighted in a press release can help distribution and exposure considerably.

Website
- Your Website
- Additional Page Links

News
- Related Stories
- Your Other Press Releases

Blogs
- Industry Blogs
- Your Blog

Your news is seen by more people online through websites, blogs and online distribution channels.

What a Press Release is NOT

A press release is not:

1. **An article:** Articles are not dated or time-sensitive. They can be published any time and they give information, not news.
2. **An opinion piece:** A press release is not your personal opinion but represents your company. Opinion pieces are best left to blogs or to the opinion page of a newspaper.
3. **A blog post:** While some people use blog software for their newsroom (which has advantages) a press release is not necessarily a blog post. Blog posts are usually more personal and informal.
4. **An advertisement:** Advertisements are centered on selling and selling alone in a press release turns people off quickly.

The goals of an online press release are several: from getting traffic to your website to sales and rankings in search engines for keyword phrases related to your business.

Don't Just Target the News Media

Don't make the mistake of putting all of your emphasis on getting a journalist to cover your story. There are fewer journalists and more people pitching to them. Journalists' jobs are being cut all of the time, as newspapers fold around the country. The reporters still working are each doing the work that several people used to do. They have less time and need to satisfy higher expectations than ever. Most hate the pitches they get from businesses because they're uninteresting and irrelevant to what they write about.

They're more likely to use a search engine or a site like Twitter to find or research a story. They increasingly rely on trusted sources of news —and ideally you'll become a source for information about your industry.

Another issue is that journalism has a high turnover. You can spend a lot of time making connections only to find that the journalist who covered your beat is gone. Then you've got to start over again. It's a lot of work to keep up with them and harder to match what they're writing about right now within your area of expertise. Journalists are a moving target. Like a regular press release, an online press release is official company communication. A press release is a formal document from your company's perspective, and is written in your corporate style. It's not a casual communication or a balanced story.

Reasons for Online Press Releases and Online PR

There are several reasons you might send out a press release or plan a PR campaign online. Most of the time the primary reason to send out a press release is to announce something.

Secondary reasons include:

Branding - getting your name out to more people online.

Reputation - creating several links to good news about your business and/or displacing negative news or stories and building trust and familiarity with your audience.

News - having a story to tell that has impact and is important to the news media.

Sales - to drive new sales or leads to your business.

Website traffic - to let people know about a new site or blog you're launching or to just get more people to your website.

Fill Search Engines with Good News about your Business

The best thing about an online press release is that it's not thrown away. Most have a permanent place in search engines. A press release increases the number of positive results about your company in search engines and can increase visibility of your business.

Social Media Press Release

A variation of an online press release is a social media press release. It's a newer form of online press releases. Basically it's written in a format that presents information in a very accessible and shareable way. You can embed graphics, RSS feeds, video, social bookmarking elements, comments and trackbacks.

PRWeb has many elements of a social media press release integrated into their system. However, for social media press releases for PR campaigns with a lot of video, audio, and images I recommend using Pitch Engine (http://www.PitchEngine.com). I've seen stories get to the top of search engines within a few days after a press release is created. However, you have to pay a monthly fee to host the press release, so its long term benefit is less unless you pay them to host the press release for you.

The website PRXBuilder.com has a free template for social media press releases. They use links and embedded content such as video and comments so people can interact with the story and pass it along rather than simply report on it.

A social media press release gives you many more tools to tell a story. For example, at a time of high home foreclosures, a social media press release may tell a story of a certain city and state and the people who face foreclosure. It could be done by a real estate team that shares how they've helped solve the issue. They could include video of people who avoided foreclosure, bookmarked stories to back up the facts, links to relevant blog posts, and pictures of neighborhoods showing several foreclosed homes on the market.

From my perspective, social media press services that host your content aren't the best long-term solutions. It's ideal if you can build your own press room on your website. Then you're building traffic to your domain and increasing the reach of your website rather than going through someone else's site. However, it can be ideal for contests or if you don't have the technical expertise or resources to build a social media press release on your own website. Also, you can benefit from the increased traffic that a social media press release site can bring.

Low Cost Compared to Other Marketing Efforts

Whatever type of online press release you choose, press releases can be an effective online marketing tool. Combined with SEO techniques, they can cost a lot less than other forms of marketing.

Build a press release that targets terms relating to your business and enjoy free traffic for much longer. Targeting specific terms will help you move up in the list of websites that come up when someone types that term into a search engine.

Companies both large and small can get great results on a modest budget with online press releases. While you still pay for distribution and exposure, it's considerably less than the cost of using a traditional news wire. With sites like PRWeb, a small business can get just as much access to major news outlets as a PR firm does.

Reporters Need Good Stories

Using the Internet you can easily research who covers what topics and for what news outlet and use that information to pitch stories to reporters. If you live in Texas, type in "Texas newspaper" to find newspapers. Then find their editorial or contact page. Most list staff and what they cover. Some magazines or newspapers have email addresses with stories. Businesswire has a helpful list of media outlets by state.

Results are Long-Lasting

A press release will drive traffic to your website from search engines long after it's released. Traffic from paid advertisements on search engines stop showing when you stop paying for the ads.

Additionally, an online press release is a form of marketing that gives information rather than pitching your products or services directly. Over time you can build visibility and trust that will pay off for years.

You Can Track Results of Press Releases

One of the best things about online press releases is your ability to track a press release and get statistics about who clicked on it, how long they spent on the page, and how they found the press release. Using that information, you can fine tune your efforts and test different headlines and copy to determine which are most effective.

Some online news distribution sites like PRWeb provide basic stats on how many people saw your headline (impressions), read it (measured by clicks to the press release), or printed your press release. PRWeb won't tell you how many people came to your website and took action (like buying something or signing up for a newsletter). For that you'll need your own web analytics.

Web Analytics Programs

Google Analytics is a free program that can tell you how people came to your website, the actions they took, and the words they typed into search engines to find you. They also tell you which websites have brought the most people to your site. This is invaluable information for you to see what is working or not working. Put your time into improving what is working.

For more details on web analytics programs, please refer to the glossary.

Twitter Tracking

To help you track results, including who has tweeted about you or your news, you can use TweetBeep (http://tweetbeep.com). You can get updates by email every hour or once a day. Set up TweetBeep so you get alerts whenever certain words are mentioned on Twitter.

Google Alerts

Another way to see how your news story is picked up is to sign up for free Google Alerts at http://www.google.com/alerts. You can track words or phrases (be sure to put them in quotes) and receive an email whenever the term is mentioned online.

Tracking Online and Offline Pickup

A site like Newspower Online can track traditional and offline PR efforts.

Ways to Measure Success

Here are ways you could measure the success of a press release or any PR effort online:

- Page views/Visits to site (note: you can get high value links to your site as a result of someone seeing a press release—even though they might link to your website and not to the press release).

- Impressions (number of times the headline was seen)

- RSS subscribers

- Leads generated

- Online revenue

- Email subscribers

- Links to the story

- Reprints of the news on portal sites (syndication)

- Stories based on your news (coverage)

- Blog posts or comments generated

- Traffic to your website

- Keyword rankings

- Conversions

You can also measure

- Social bookmarks or friends on social sites

Radian6 (http://www.radian6.com) is a paid service that helps you keep track of social mentions. You can see who the influencers are in your space too.

This simple link popularity tool can be used to see the number of links your press release or web page get—just by typing in the URL: http://www.webmaster-toolkit.com/link-popularity-checker.shtml.

Just remember that quantity is only one measurement. Even if you don't get a huge response, your campaign can be successful by reaching influential people in your industry. The relationships you make can pay off long after a PR campaign ends.

Tracking Sales from a Press Release:
Case Study—Southwest Airlines

This is a famous case of how one press release can be directly traced to tens of thousands in revenue.

In 2004, Southwest Airlines published a press release about a fare sale. It was written about in major newspapers like the New York Times. The press release ranked #1 for the term "airfare to Philadelphia" for at least the next month.

The press release was tied to a unique landing page and the sale wasn't offered anywhere else. At first it generated $42,000 and over time it made Southwest over $80,000.[1]

To see how many total links your press release got in a search engine, simply type the title with quotes around it into any search engine. On the upper left it will list the total number of websites with that title. Be aware that this isn't usually a complete list but a sampling.

---

1. http://tinyurl.com/qjo8xm
instituteforpr.org/files/uploads/SWA_Measurement.pdf

Traffic, not Necessarily Press

Online PR has a different focus than most press releases. Most businesses want reporters to call and to see their company on the pages of newspapers, magazines, or on the nightly news. Certainly, that is a possibility. A press release can lead to press coverage, but most do not. Still, a press release distributed online can provide the benefit of building links to your website, selling directly to your customers, appearing on blogs, and getting more recognition. In that sense, the Internet can outweigh the benefit of getting stories in traditional media outlets.

Getting a story on the nightly news and getting coverage online can both happen with online news distribution. That is the real power of online press releases.

Short Term Benefits of a Press Release

Initially, the first thing a new client often sees is a large bump in traffic to their website the day the press release is distributed. Then after looking at their web stats, they'll often see that a single press release continues to bring people in, referring new people to their site. Pay one time; get benefits from then on. It's a great model.

Many clients say they get 50% more traffic to their website in the first day or two after they send out a press release.

Long Term Benefits of an Online Press Release

Press releases can provide links to your website and help your site build a strong reputation online. Companies need to be aware of how they're perceived online. Once a negative review or comment about a business reaches the first pages of a search engine, it can be tough to remove. The longer the search result has been there, the harder it can be to displace. So filling search results with company news from press releases is part of reputation management. It helps to have positive results from a variety of sources.

NOTE: According to Advertising Age, PR firms have published paid ads to respond to negative news or promote positive news. The ads link to a page or blog post with more information. You can do the same. The ad should go to a page on your website or a blog post with more information.

Advertising Options (choose an option that will reach your targeted audience online):

TwitterHawk - You pay five cents a click for ads that run on Twitter.

PayPerClick Ads through Google, Yahoo, and MSN.

Facebook Ads - The ads can be very targeted, cost-effective and easy to set up.

Another benefit is the permanent link in search engines that can help your business rank highly on terms that are important to your business.

Why can't I just put the press release on my corporate website and/or blog and call it good?

I recommend that you put most or all press releases on your website and blog about them. Some say all you need is a blog. However, news distribution services like PRWeb (the foremost online press distribution site) have a much larger, wider distribution than most business blogs or corporate websites. You'll reach additional audiences that you can't reach on your own.

Getting media coverage is important because it earns you credibility that advertising can't. When writing a press release, being unique and timely is vital.

The more newsworthy you make your stories, the more coverage you'll get. Some companies, (such as Ancestry.com) have been so effective at getting media coverage that some reporters almost refuse to run another story about them. Luckily, there are so many outlets and potential stories online that you shouldn't have to worry about this problem.

As important as getting your news is to establish yourself as a trusted, credible business. If you don't have a lot of visibility, find people who do and get to know them.

A press release is a chance to show your company's human side but it's still a formal document. It's more formal than blog posts and other communication online. Most companies use them to brag or to appear important (sometimes even to spin or misrepresent).

A Note About Publicly Traded Companies

News announcements from publicly traded companies are different than those from privately held companies. For this I asked David Politis, President of Draper, Utah-based Politis Communications and a 25-year public relations and investor relations professional for direction.

"The rules are different for companies with shares traded on a public stock exchange like NASDAQ or the New York Stock Exchange," Politis said. "The SEC (Securities and Exchange Commission) is concerned that all potential buyers and sellers of stock have equal access to important, breaking news at the same time. That's known as Fair Disclosure of *material news*, and in the world of the SEC, information is considered *material* if that information is not yet public and the average investor would see that information as a reason to buy or sell stock."

The risk for publicly traded companies, Politis went on to explain, is that if they do not use a wire service to distribute their *material news*, some investors may have access to that news before others. Such actions would put those companies in violation of the Securities Acts of 1933 and 1934, as well as Regulation Fair Disclosure, which can lead to fines and penalties, including an SEC or stock exchange ordered halt in trading.

"That's why you almost always see publicly traded companies use a commercial wire service to distribute press releases," Politis added, which is exactly what Politis Communications advises its public clients to do. "Besides, the bigger wire services automatically feed news releases right into the private monitors and systems used by stock brokers, investment bankers and fund managers, which means new news can be instantly flagged for financial professionals following particular companies."

"Releases distributed via wire services can also have a very strong and long-term SEO value for companies. These are just some of the reasons why we still recommend companies use a commercial wire service when distributing news releases—almost always for publicly traded companies and selectively for privately held companies."

For the record, Politis Communications prefers Business Wire, but it has also used PR Newswire and PRWeb.

David also mentioned that you should consider distributing press releases online and using social media long before you go public. If you've been participating for a year or two before you go public, then it will be part of your marketing strategy. Beginning online marketing like this after declaring your intention to go public can be seen by regulators as interfering in the process of going public.

Be Transparent

People will call you out on lies, and negative comments can spread and travel fast. Be honest about who you are and what you're doing. Don't try to fake something just for news value. It could backfire.

Approaches to Online Press Releases

You can take existing press releases from your PR firm or some that you've written for your website. Optimize and distribute them through an online press release distribution site. Then blog about and social bookmark/share that press release online. Make a strategy to decide the level of news and which services to use.

Minor News

You can distribute press releases for free or around $50 mostly for the search engine benefit. If it's minor news, go for keyword placement and choose a free site or a low cost site like 24-7pressrelease.com. There is a list of free sites in Appendix C.

Example: New hires, speaking at minor conferences, small awards, minor partnerships, promotions, etc. The goal for minor news is to get links to your site with keyword phrases.

Bigger News

If it's bigger news that has a strong story or if you want to add extra features like video, choose a more comprehensive service like PRWeb. Take the time to email journalists and bloggers about the story.

This is news that you should focus more promotion efforts on, which I'll reference later.

Make News Fun

Try to inject some fun into your news release, when it fits. Hold a contest. Ask people to write about, tweet about, bookmark or respond to you to be entered into the contest. Hold a drawing for those who participate. Actively solicit participation in your newsletter and other marketing efforts. Be sure to blog and Tweet about the contest before, during and after it ends.

The goal is to get links and media coverage and to spread the news to bloggers and on social networks.

Chapter 1: Online Press Releases Defined

Chapter

2 | Online PR Defined

Don Middleberg coined the term 'Online PR' in 2001 and attempted to claim the Internet back then for the PR industry. He pointed out that PR is about a brilliant idea communicated through various forms of media and online was the next form.
Salesvantage.com

Seth Godin is a master at marketing online because he understands that it's better to pull your customers to you than to push your message to them. He says:

PR is the strategic crafting of your story. It's the focused examination of your interactions and tactics and products and pricing that, when combined, determine what and how people talk about you.

With online PR you take your story, interaction, and tactics online. There are people communicating all of the time and you can view and join those conversations.

Where traditional PR is used to influence broadcast and print media (papers, magazines, radio, TV, and so on) online PR influences your reputation with online. There are ways to combine online and offline media to extend the reach of your campaigns. Often a successful PR campaign starts online and is then picked up by traditional media rather than the other way around.

Here are some key ways online PR differs from traditional PR:

- Online it's much more of a conversation than a one-way communication.

- The tone is usually more conversational and casual.

- People can and are likely to respond (negatively or otherwise) to your marketing efforts. Sometimes the backlash can be harsh (just ask Motrin who angered moms with this controversial video http://www.youtube.com/watch?v=BmykFKjNpdY). You can see what people said about it on Twitter at http://search.twitter.com/search?q=motrin+moms or http://hashtags.org/tag/Motrinmoms.

- You have to give up control of the message because people can and will change it and voice their opinions. All opinions will not be positive.

- Things happen fast and negative news or free food promotions can get big within minutes or hours.

- Online PR requires more technical skills and as it gets more advanced may even require specialized programming skills.

- Online PR has its own terms and methods.

Demand for online PR is rising and it requires different skills than traditional PR—usually more technical skills. Talk to anyone in PR and they'll tell you how much they've been influenced by the Internet. All marketing has been. And, like the newspaper industry, the grim truth is that for most, the choice is to either adapt or have your business die.

More people are getting news online and from each other rather from watching the news on television. Sites like Twitter can deliver news before traditional channels and individuals are reporting news directly rather than waiting to read about it or hear about it on the news.

In coming years more people will be on social networking sites. Since 2005, the number of people on these sites has risen dramatically. People with strong online networks have more reach than ever. That reach will continue to grow.

According to the Pew Internet & American Life Project:

> "The share of adult internet users who have a profile on an online social network site has more than quadrupled in the past four years—from 8% in 2005 to 35% now, according to the Pew Internet & American Life Project's December 2008 tracking survey."[2]

Just recently more people have reported that they use search engines as much or more than the Yellow Pages to find local businesses.[3]

People Have More Control Over the News

It's important to understand the lack of control you have over the medium. People are more in control and they decide how, where, and when to get information online. It's much easier to guide a story that only reaches a few, but when it goes to the public they can respond to, add to, and modify the story in unexpected ways.

We live in an ADD world which means people have short attention spans and are doing many things at once. That means you've got to be engaging!

---

2. http://tinyurl.com/d4g93e
pewinternet.org/Reports/2009/Adults-and-Social-Network-Web-sites.aspx

3. http://tinyurl.com/mrof65
smallbiztrends.com/2008/12/not-just-the-yellow-pages-any-more-how-people-find-local-businesses.htm

3 The Newswires

The two biggest traditional newswire services are PRNewswire and Business Wire. Both have introduced services for smaller budgets through partner sites that I reference at the end of this book. The wires distribute to journalists and major news outlets like the New York Times. Pricing is varied and usually requires a subscription. Unless you choose the right package they don't include SEO or social media benefits.

PRWeb offers Business Wire services through PRWeb Direct.

Business Wire has over 40 years of experience and is affiliated with over 60 news services. News can be targeted to particular cities or countries or distributed worldwide to more than 100 industries.

PRNewswire clients include some 40,000 corporate, government, association, labor, and non-profit organizations worldwide, and they maintain offices in 14 countries. A press release managed by PR Newswire can be sent to 135 countries in 30 different languages. Customers get 24/7 customer support and feedback evaluating the success of each release.

Online News Distribution Sites

PRWeb is the industry-leading online press release service. It provides a variety of services to a range of customers from those who have just started their business to Fortune 500 companies. It was bought by Vocus in 2006. In addition to Google News, Yahoo News, and other sites, PRWeb sends over 14 million outbound emails a day to journalists. Their press releases are also featured on partner sites and blogs.

Ninety-five per cent of their email addresses are to individual "opt-in" journalists who have supplied their personal email addresses (at the personal request of the journalist) rather than sending to a generic email such as editor@newsroom.com.

There are many other sites with fewer features but equally good SEO benefits for very reasonable prices (under $50).
Clickpress (http://www.clickpress.com),
24-7pressrelease (http://www.24-7pressrelease.com), and
PRLeap (http://www.prleap.com) are my favorites.

There are many free sites which I review and there are a few worth noting. It may be beneficial to submit a press release to free sites in addition to paid sites.

Associated Press, Reuter's, etc.

Traditional news services like the Associated Press (AP) are offline-focused. They gather and distribute news to their members. AP is owned by newspapers, radio, and television stations. They both contribute stories and use material written by AP staff journalists (here's a US map showing AP stories by state). They do not accept press releases.

Services that claim exposure to these wires usually email a list of headlines to AP reporters. The updates they send are very short—just a sentence or two about the news. These organizations send reporters to cover news stories around the world and members pay a fee to access the stories, pictures, and video.

Online press release services don't produce news—they distribute it on the Internet and don't charge for people to reprint it. In fact, the more people link to the news, the better.

Best Websites to Send an Online Press Release

According to Internet Marketing Rankings for June 2009, on topseos.com website, the 10 top companies in the category of Press Release Distribution are:[4]

1. PRWeb
2. Business Wire (a traditional wire service with online/SEO features. Also available through PRWeb's PRWebDirect service)
3. Market Wire (a traditional wire service with online/SEO features)
4. 24-7pressrelease.com
5. PR.com
6. PRLeap
7. eReleases.com
8. PRNewswire
9. Eworldwire
10. Rush PR News

An Alexa Traffic History Graph of website traffic for these five companies for six months ending March 2009 shows PRWeb at the top of that list. In light of the claim by PRWeb that they are the leader of online newswire services, this data appears to confirm that they are indeed the current leader in press release marketing.

---

4. See the entire list at: http://tinyurl.com/d97zxb. topseos.com/rankings-of-best-press-release-distribution-companies

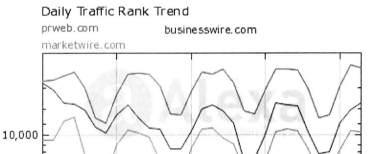

Alexa ranking for some of the top rated online press release distribution websites.

4 Be Newsworthy

If you want to get the maximum benefit from your press release, it's got to be newsworthy. What makes something newsworthy? You must have something interesting enough to say that someone would care. You have to have a good story. Finding something newsworthy to say is the beginning of a successful press release. It's also something many businesses struggle to do.

If you catch something on the news that relates to your business, send out a press release right away. Being first to respond with your story can get you great coverage.

This is what Larry Weaver, of Funny Employee Awards (http://www.funnyemployeeawards.com) learned when he identified a trend and became the expert on it:

> In late summer of 2008, I sent a press release online through PRNewswire.com. In the release, I made the statement that cancelling corporate Christmas parties were becoming a disturbing trend because of the economy. As it turned out, companies cancelling Christmas parties became big news later in the year.

Because I had made the call so early on, a lot of journalists found my press release and regarded me as an authority on the subject. This led to two interviews from Associated Press reporters. Both of those articles ended up getting picked up in major newspapers across the world. That exposure multiplied further into additional exposure. All of this because I sent a press release identifying a trend that others had not yet picked up on. Reporters want news. If you spot a trend, online press releases are a great way to brand yourself as an expert.

Remember news is not just information—it exists in time: either something has happened (sales for new homes are up), something will happen in the future (a future event you're sponsoring), or something is happening now (a trend). News has an expiration date and is timely. If all you have is information that can be shared anytime, write an article.

People won't care about your news unless it relates to what they are writing about right now. Most people should spend a lot of time deciding on what to write about first and then the story you're going to tell about it. Your news might be about how you're going to be at a trade show. That's news. To get a *story*, find something interesting about being at the tradeshow.

Ask a lot of questions. Think of what a reporter might ask you and answer those questions. Is your business focus shifting to a new area? If so, why? What is going on in your industry? What do you hope to do there or accomplish? Is there someone notable who will be at your booth? Dig for something that tells an interesting story.

People often make the mistake of thinking their brand or product is important just because. It's easy to be enamoured with your product or company but not everyone will be. Always think of your customers or the community and how you can benefit them and you'll be more effective than trying to tell others how great you are.

Chapter 4: Be Newsworthy

Ideas for Newsworthy Press Releases

- You just created a new social media profile or blog. This includes a Facebook, or Twitter. Be sure to add the URLs to all of your social media sites. Tell people what your goal with the site is and topics covered. Do you give out deals, highlight specials, give good information or reviews? Use this to invite people to become your friend or follower. Consider giving an incentive for those who do (like a free guide).

- You launched an affiliate program. Be sure to give some of the details that stand out like the cookie duration, payout, introduce the affiliate manager, and the network you'll be on.

- You were recognized in a top publication or on a popular television, magazine, or radio show. Include a link to video or audio to the story if you have it.

- You're speaking at an event.

- You have a unique perspective on the news right now—a local slant or a new approach.

- You have a new product or service or an important feature has been added to an existing product or service. Tell people how to use it and why you created it.

- Anything creative you're doing for marketing that is buzz-worthy.

- New research and/or trends from you or your industry. Relate them back to what you do. Give commentary.

- You have success stories from customers illustrating a common theme (this usually helps you see what you're doing best—publicize it).

- You were especially successful on a marketing campaign, speech, etc.

- Your CEO did an interview or will do one. Tell people what they'll learn and then send one to recap the response if it was especially strong.

- Write about seasonal specials or sales (back to school, holidays, season).

- Top tips tied into a current trend, i.e. right now the recession is forcing people to economize. Any story that gives ways to save money or to earn extra money are popular right now.

- Use Google Insights (http://www.google.com/insights/search) for search to see what's hot in your industry. See what news there is. Write about it from your perspective.

- Announce new partnerships or sponsors. Recognize what they bring to the business. Check with the partner to review before sending.

- Look at your website stats and see what common searches people are doing. Search for questions starting with "How to" or "Why" and write a press release answering a common question.

- Write if you supported a good cause or were part of a campaign to help a good cause or a non-profit.

- You won a big award or got recognized for achievements.

- You have a creative solution to a problem or found a new use for your product. For example, a baby sign language company finds success in China helping adults learn English.

When possible include links, images audio, and video.

Here are some tips to find a good story or angle:
http://www.russpage.net/pr-tips/

Look for a Good Angle

I wrote a press release for someone who markets a backup service for bloggers who want to back up their blog. Boring. That was going to be the main focus—that you could back up your blog—until I asked some more questions and found out why the business was started.

Here's the story: the owner's wife lost her personal blog that she poured hours into writing it over several years. Her husband came up with the idea to provide a service for people like her who need to be sure their blog is backed up. Losing all that work is something many bloggers can relate to. We put so much into our blog and losing that would be devastating. That was the story, and it got better coverage than if it had just been an announcement about a new service for bloggers.

Tell your story first; talk about your company next. Try to tell a story that connects with people. Any marketer will tell you that most people buy more on emotion than logic. Do what you can to connect with your audience and then tell them about your business.

Shoemoney Case Study

I wrote a press release for Shoemoney (Shoemoney is the name of popular tech blogger Jeremy Shoemaker's blog). The story started out being about a fundraiser and mostly about the company that sponsored the event. It was a run to raise money for a nonprofit. I took the news and made it into a bigger story about a man who was a soldier and now a champion boxer who wanted to help military families in crisis.

I wanted to see if I could get a perfect 5/5 editorial score and get the best coverage possible. When a member of the media signs up to get PRWeb's press release by email they can filter them in various ways. One way is filter them by quality by specifying the minimum editorial score. Getting a higher rating means more people will see the press release.

NOTE: PRWeb has since stopped giving editorial scores.

Jeremy wanted to get media exposure so the story had to be strong. I took the emphasis from the company sponsoring the fundraiser (Fighters.com) and put it on the human element. That is the families and their financial struggles at home. It had emotional pull. The fundraiser became an answer to a problem. At that point people cared more about the company addressing the issue.

It is tempting to brag or to sing your product's praises, but then it looks like an advertisement. So I removed all the bragging and led with the story—that the families of troops are struggling and the company is holding a race to raise money.

I ended up getting a perfect score and the business got great exposure. It wasn't what the client expected, but it worked. It also brought me a lot of new business.

Old headline: Fighters.com Sponsors the Xtreme Couture Operation Freedom Run

New headline: Nonprofit Organizes Run in Vegas to Raise Funds for US Soldiers in Financial Crisis

I started with the headline. It was about the run only. I rewrote it to talk about the central message—which was that military families need help. Next, I removed all the bragging and self-promotion. If you have a good story people will contact you and that's when you can tell them more. I wanted to widen the scope and reach people who had never heard about Shoemoney, Fighters, or the run. Because first off, it's really about the soldiers who are in crisis.

Here's what Shoemoney said about the press release:

I was on 4 radio stations and in 2 newspapers and had inquiries from a TON of media sources. Janet had been able to score another perfect prweb score and had incredible distribution for my press release.

Shoemoney wrote this about it on his blog. (This post brought me new business for several months even though it was mentioned at the end of his post. It wasn't the topic of the entire post. This illustrates the power of reaching bloggers who have a lot of trust built with their audiences.)

We had invested a lot of money in a charity event for fighters.com and I wanted to get some good exposure with an awesome press release. I twittered asking for a prweb ninja who can get 5's and great distribution. @prweb responded with Newspapergrl aka Janet Meiners. So I wrote her an email asking how much she would charge. I will be honest when I first saw the press release she did I was not that impressed. I am a branding guy and I did not feel like our company was mentioned enough. She was really focusing on the event. She said to trust her and that she knew what she was doing. Fair enough (I love confident people).

Then a couple days later my phone was ringing off the hook (no joke). I was on 4 radio stations and in two news papers and had inquiries from a TON of media sources. Janet had been able to score another perfect prweb score and had incredible distribution for my press release. [5]

How to Come up with Newsworthy Ideas

There are obvious things to write a press release about. Announce new products, a new blog, major hires, awards, events, success stories or even that you've joined Facebook or Twitter.

There are many ways to come up with newsworthy ideas. It helps to look at press releases from other businesses that reach a similar audience. Search these sites on a particular topic to come up with new stories or angles for your press releases.

Here are some sources I regularly consult when I start a new press release and need inspiration or insight.

Online News Websites

Look at news sites (like PRWeb or AP stories) to get ideas for news and how news is worded. Do a search on a news site for a related word and scan the headlines. Look for possible angles or perspectives. It

---

5. http://tinyurl.com/porbhr
shoemoney.com/2008/06/02/how-do-you-choose-who-to-hire-and-why-not-remote

doesn't even need to be in your industry. Just seeing what news interests you about a topic will provide insight into what you could write about. Notice who is doing well and learn from their work.

HARO

Sign up for the Help a Reporter Out (HARO) at http://www.helpareporter.com email list and use it to do research and see the perspective of reporters. Three times a day HARO sends an email with pitches from reporters and bloggers who are looking for stories they're writing. The pitches come from different publications, individuals looking for case studies for their book, and everything in between. The pitches come from unknowns to the biggest news outlets in the country.

Quickly skim or search each email to get an idea what people are writing about. Each pitch has a summary of the angle the reporter is taking on the news. Use HARO to see what news topics are popular right now and what information or angles reporters are pursuing. See if you can come up with an angle that fits your business.

Last count they had 42,000 sources (people who signed up to get pitches from reporters who are writing stories in hopes that they will be quoted in stories) and 7,500 journalists on the email list.

Google Insights for Search
(http://www.google.com/insights/search)

Google has a tool that is helpful for online press releases. It shows you the trends of web searches and offers many ways to filter results. You can get online news stories plotted on a graph correlated with search volume.

You can search for a topic by time (within the past 18 months), category (health, sports, etc.), and other filters. See rising or declining demand based on number of searches.

At the bottom of the page, you can see related keywords and the top rising keywords. You can also search by geographic area—so you can see what local markets or areas of the world are hot for your news topic. Use that information to see what is popular and to test different keywords.

TrendHunter (www.trendhunter.com)

This is a website that spots trends. Use it to get ideas for your business based on what's hot. Then come up with a way to tie your story into a national story and instantly expand your audience. This is a good way to get higher score on PRWeb and therefore enjoy better distribution. The most efficient way to keep up on trends is to sign up for TrendHunter's email newsletter.

Seasons, Weather, Holidays, Elections

When it's back-to-school, try to tie your business into this rite of passage. When it's cold, announce your new line of sweaters. At Christmas, talk about how your business is preparing for the holidays (specials, give people a top 10 gift list, come up with suggestions on how to celebrate the holidays with your products, etc.).

At election time you can tie your business or product into the candidates, issues, or political party. These are cyclical topics that become newsworthy. Keep them in mind as you plan your campaigns.

Create Your Own News

If you can't come up with news, you can always create it. This is the fun part because you can be creative and it's usually the more outlandish ideas that catch on and get passed around online (go viral). Many times this is the best type of news because it has an element of fun.

BlendTec's wildly popular "Will it Blend?" series is a great example. There are many stories about how it came to be. The version I've heard is that it started at a company meeting when the CEO was showing employees how durable their blenders are. He grabbed golf clubs and put them into a blender. The blender turned the clubs into powder. Everyone loved it and started talking about it.

This became the basis of videos of blending unlikely items from glow sticks to iPods. The videos were put on YouTube and shared in different ways. There are over 20 videos that have had almost 40 million views on YouTube and iPhones. Combined, their videos have been viewed over 100 million times.

The reason this idea spread so fast was not because they had a news story about how great their blenders are. It spread because they had a fun idea and they used social media to showcase it. They didn't say but they showed that their blenders could handle just about anything. The videos were authentic. Could you start a video series about your product?

Here are examples of publicity that people have created to get buzz or create news (http://tinyurl.com/ca6u7t).

Example: 7–11 Election

The convenience store 7–11 has gotten a lot of press and visibility for their 7-Election campaign. Around election time, customers can get their coffee in a red Republican cup or a blue Democrat cup. The cup you choose is your vote. Interestingly enough, America's coffee buying habits have often predicted recent election results. If more blue cups sell that year, it's likely the Democrats will win. If more red cups sell, it's likely to be a Republican victory. They set up a website to track the voting.

Pictures of the cups and stories about the game are all over the Internet and blogs. They got incredible media and online coverage for the story. Here's the press release: http://tinyurl.com/mvu826.

Over 350,00 people voted in the "Dewmocracy." The new flavor, Voltage, made the news. The people who participated were also most likely some of the first customers to buy the new drink. Involving your customers in your marketing campaign online is a smart marketing tactic. It's a way to build a fan base and pre-market a product.

Example: The PR Road Trip: How A Car Website Got $92,000 in PR for next to Nothing

Chris Hedgecock started http://www.carsforagrand.com which is basically a website featuring cars selling on eBay for under $1,000. He wanted to show that in a recession you don't have to spend on an expensive car. You can buy a reliable car for very little.

He got an idea to generate some press—buy a car from his site and take it on road trip. He bought a $900 Pontiac off his site and drove it from San Diego to Miami. In the process got a lot of press. He had his domain name in vinyl lettering across the side of his car.

Here's what he said:

"I thought it would be a great idea to buy a car for under $1,000 from the site and drive it coast to coast in an attempt to get some news coverage and visitors to the site. **We were successful in appearing on a dozen news broadcasts and driving almost half a million visitors to the site in three weeks—all for free.**

On the largest day we did over 110,000 uniques [or new visitors to his website]—all for free. Not to say it wasn't a lot of work, but it was also a lot of fun."

While he didn't hire a PR firm, he did get friends involved (and he has good contacts who had the know-how). I wouldn't say it was free but it was definitely less than he could've spent running ads—and much more effective.

Elements of Success:

- A personality and attitude, Chris likes meeting people (being social). He was willing to be creative and then do what it took to accomplish what he was after.

- Time. Notice he drove across the country and planned all of this—lots and lots of time. He wasn't sitting in his office. He followed up a and kept track of things. He took the time to make the story relevant to the local market he was in.

- Know-how. He learned or knew how to create a YouTube channel, video, blog, etc. If you don't have this, you can learn or pay someone for consulting.

- Contacts. His friend did a lot of legwork. He had someone write and distribute press releases to get local coverage at every major city along the trip.

- His blog documented the journey with video, images, and updates.

Chris used News Power, a website to help track results. They estimated the news value of his press was over $92,000!

This is a great example of the power of online marketing and PR. Chris generated links and content that will last far longer online than the road trip. In other words, it's a campaign that will continue to bring new people to his site. He also had fun, which is a great way to attract attention.

If you have more examples of successful online PR campaigns, I hope you'll share them with me at http://www.newspapergrl.com/contact or email janet@affililateflash.com I will blog about them and highlight them in my marketing to help increase their exposure. With your permission I may use your story in another book.

Other things you can do to create news:

Put a billboard on Google Earth (and send out a press release with a picture of it and link to it).
http://blog.futurelab.net/2007/02/billboards_in_google_earth.html

Put a picture on Google's Picasa and tag it with a specific location and it will show up on Google Earth.

Expand Relevancy and Get Bigger Coverage by Tying your News into a Bigger Trend

When your story is based on your local market, you have a chance of getting picked up by a local news source or on local searches. Expanding a local phenomenon or news into a larger trend can turn a limited story into a story that can get picked up nationwide.

The '2009 Social Media Marketing and PR Benchmark Guide' from MarketingSherpa said the following: "Rather than creating content around what you think will be popular, create it around what is already popular." This is great advice.

Use the Internet to see what is popular and join the conversations, starting with putting out a news release about your business. It also means you're relevant—and relevancy is key online.

PRWeb grades the quality of a press release on a scale from one to five. When someone signs up to get an email digest from PRWeb they choose press releases by choosing the editorial score. They can get press releases with a 4 or higher score. What that means to you: the higher the score, the more people will see your press release.

Example: Expanding the Story of a Real Estate Press Release

A real estate company had a well-written press release about how more sellers in a particular city were hosting their own open houses. Homes were on the market longer and sellers were looking for ways to find potential buyers. This is a story playing out across the country.

The press release had quotes and antidotes from local real estate agents about techniques that were successful. I rewrote the press release so it had a national appeal while keeping the local keywords (or keywords that name a city and/or state, such as "Seattle Washington real estate"). It tied into a housing trend across the nation—that homes are not selling as quickly and sellers were getting creative in an effort to sell faster.

I shared tips for successful open houses in a tough housing market. It got a perfect 5 editorial score. The story went from being about one area to a story that applied to many places in the country experiencing similar conditions.

NOTE: This is the part the most people struggle with the most—coming up with a good story. When you have a good story, proceed to back it up with strong quotes and information to prove the point.

Email Interviews

One of my favorite ways to develop a story is to interview key people in the story by email. I think of a list of questions that someone who is educated but not familiar with the business might ask. This is where I get to be the reporter.

I ask people who are experts or key to the story questions such as:

- What is the significance of this news?

- Who does it affect and why?

- How does it benefit your customers?

- How did this idea originate—who thought of it and why?

- Do you have any stories or case studies from your clients to illustrate your point?

- Do you have any research, stats or anecdotes to support your claims?

- Who are you trying to target in this news release?

- What action would you like them to take?

- What unique qualifications do you have relating to the news?

And so on...then I use their answers in the press release and as quotes. It's an efficient way to cover every angle and get great quotes. Plus I never have to worry about misquoting because it's in their own words.

5 Write for the Internet—How it's Different

In the past, companies could get away with sending press releases that almost no one would read. Reporters could toss them and that was the end. But online, your press releases live on and anyone can read them. Unfortunately, companies will always churn out boring press releases that you couldn't pay anyone to read.

Like blogging, online press releases benefit from having an honest and authentic style. Remember that your press release has many audiences, and not all are familiar with your industry, products, or business.

With online PR people read your press release on a computer screen or on mobile device screens. The Internet has changed how people read information. We skim information for the main points. We tend to multitask and be doing many things at one time. We're impatient. We want to get the story and why it matters quickly. If we don't get that, we're on to something else.

Here are some tips to writing online:

1. Use short sentences. Long sentences are difficult to follow. If your sentence gets long, break it up into two or more sentences. I'm

not sure why but people often make the first sentence of a press release unnaturally long.

2. Keep paragraphs short. It's easier on the eyes to have white space. Start a new paragraph every 1–4 sentences.

3. Don't use clichés, jargon or buzz words. They turn people off. Avoid this oft-abused phrase as a quote..."we're excited to announce." Instead of saying you're excited, tell what is exciting about the news.

4. Use straightforward language. Write at the 6th grade level and link to or be available to offer more detailed information.

5. No bragging. If you must brag, do it through stats, quotes from other people, or research. Also remember that words you use and are familiar with in your industry could have totally different meanings to another industry.

6. Are you trying to look good? It's not all about you. Instead think: How can I help or contribute to the conversation or community? What information would be helpful to someone reading this?

7. Keep it simple and cut out the fluff. Hyperbole makes people suspicious (for example, "This sounds too good to be true...").

8. Be specific. Give specific examples, data, or and use precise words to tell the most important points of the story. An "appliance" might be a stove in your kitchen but to an IT guy it's something else and to a dentist... you get the idea. Search engines can't always tell the difference unless you use descriptive words.

9. Get to the point—quickly. People often read a headline, read the caption under a photo, or scan quotes in seconds. If you don't capture their attention, they're gone.

10. Use headings and bullet points, and summarize main points.

11. Link to your website, and authority sites for more information.

Here are some more press release tips from PRWeb:
http://www.prwebdirect.com/pressreleasetips.php

A press release announcing a new website isn't usually newsworthy enough to get good coverage, but occasionally it is. For example, online dating site eHarmony was sued for not allowing gays and lesbians to use their online dating website. They launched a new website just for homosexuals. That new site is newsworthy and the press release about it was interesting. Most press releases about new sites aren't.

Headlines

Here are five headline writing tips with examples:

1. **Play up the underdog story.**
   People like to root for the little guy—the David facing the Goliath. The coupon site FatWallet took on Walmart after they threatened to sue the site for publishing Black Friday deals before they were released to the public. It got a lot of media attention. When a small business takes on bigger business, it can make great news.

2. **Use Numbers.**
   AP style dictates that you spell out numbers. But studies have shown that using numerals rather than spelling out a number is more effective. Even if you use a number below 10, you do not have to spell it out if you are writing primarily for the web.

3. **Make a list.**
   This is one of my favorites (note: needs to be newsworthy too). Examples: 10 Ways To Stop Gaining Weight During the Holidays, 5 Surefire Tactics to Get Media Attention, The 2 Worst Mistakes PR Firms Make, etc.

4. **Play to controversy.**
   Remember Proposition 8—the amendment to end gay marriage in California? It got a lot of attention because it's so controversial. People have strong opinions both ways. It was in the news for weeks after the election. Your unique opinion on an issue like this can get you noticed.

5. **Piggyback on current news, bigger names or events.**
   Let's say that the women's gym Curves was in the news and you owned a gym called Absolute Women Fitness (or the name of another company that owned a gym for women).

   You could write a press release like this: Who helps women lose more weight—Curves or Absolute Fitness? You can put yourself into a much bigger conversation by associating yourself with bigger names and news. Use the names of celebrities or more well-known competitors.

6. Solve a problem, make something more simple, save people time or money.
   This is a classic tactic. Right now any story about the economy or saving money can be hot.

Most of the time, write a negative headline rather than a positive one. They often work best. Your headline could be on "how NOT to" do something or how to avoid disaster. This is often more motivating than pointing out how to do something right.

6 Search Engine Optimizing a Press Release

In a survey of small businesses of fewer than 100 people, the number one rated marketing tactic in terms of effectiveness is SEO. **Good content is part of good SEO.**

When you create useful content, you are creating something that people want to know about, will link to, and will share. The more quality links you have to your press release or pages on your site the better your search engine rankings will be.

You just have to make it easy for people to find and share your content. With all the web pages to look through if you're not using SEO you practically don't exist. No matter how great your press release or other content is, people have to be able to find it.

That's what a well-distributed press releases can do quite wel—give you more visibility. It will give you a wider audience of people who are looking for news like yours.

Good content is also the basis of good marketing. Thanks to the Internet you don't have to guess what people want to know—you can ask them or uncover it. You can search forums and see what people are asking or talking about. You can use search.twitter.com. You can look at blogs or use any of the tools I discussed previously.

Another foundation of marketing online is using keywords in your content. Here's a good primer on how it works: http://tinyurl.com/pzfuzm.

Identify Keywords

Keywords are words, or more often a string of words or a phrase that someone uses to find pages when conducting a search on the Internet.

Before you write a press release, do some research to see what words or phrases relate to your news, industry or brand. Effective keywords are not guessed or made up, but researched.

You can find out what people are typing in by looking at your own web stats or by consulting a keyword tool. Start out with a generic word, like shoes and it will give you back all sorts of combination of the word. It also gives you an idea of the number of searches the phrase gets.

Start by brainstorming a list of words that describe you, your business, your product or service featured in your news. Then use the keyword tool to find one to six related keyword phrases. These will be the foundation of your press release and online PR efforts for this piece of news.

Another way to find keywords is to look at domains that rank high in search engines for topics relating to your business. Google's keyword tool (https://adwords.google.com/select/KeywordToolExternal) will extract keywords from your website or another site. Simply choose the option that says to get your keyword ideas from your website content. Then put in your website URL. It will return a list of terms with their relative demand and competition.

Another simple keyword tool that gives you an idea of keyword phrases is http://freekeywords.wordtracker.com. Keep in mind that it doesn't include results from Google so the actual numbers of searches per month are likely much higher than the numbers shown.

People often make the mistake of choosing very competitive keywords that everyone else is targeting. Your chances of ranking well on those terms are low if you're just starting out. You'll be much more effective if you use keywords that have less competition—but also have demand. These are usually longer, more specific terms rather than short generic terms.

Using one word as a keyword is hardly ever effective. The word "shoes" will have a lot of searches but will be so competitive that you'll do better to focus on a specific type of shoes. A phrase like "women's running shoes" stands a better chance of ranking well. Almost all one-word keywords will be far too competitive, so avoid them and use phrases instead.

Local keywords are also effective if your business serves a local area, such as a restaurant that has a specific physical location or a photographer who works in specific cities. To focus on local traffic, put a city name or state in front of the keyword phrase. If you own a shoe store in Houston, Texas, you can insert the city and/or state name in front of the phrase. Rather than "women's running shoes" it could be "Houston women's running shoes."

On search engines, abbreviations, acronyms, plural, and singular words will each have separate results. Start out by brainstorming all of the possible words people may use to describe your product, business, or service. Or, focus on words that you know work or that you're already targeting.

Once you identify what keyword phrases or related keywords you want to target, you should use those keywords in specific ways. You want your press release to come up on the first page of results when someone types that phrase into a search engine. This also helps the pages you link to (your own website) in search results.

Use a keyword tool to discover how people are looking for your products or services. In this example, are people searching by brand name, type of shoe (jogging shoe, dress shoe, etc.), or who the shoe is for (babies, women, men, basketball players, runners, etc.)?

Avoid one-word keywords that are almost always too competitive. The word "shoe" might have a lot of searches but it will also have more competition. It can be effective to focus on keyword phrases that don't get as many searches but will be easier to rank for.

To get an idea of competition, put the following into the Google search box:

Allintitle: "keyword phrase"

Then look on the top right hand side to see the number of sites that come up. These are people who are specifically targeting that phrase by using it in the title of their site. Since that's one of the most important ways a search engine can tell what a web page is about, it's a good measure of competition for a keyword phrase.

Make a spreadsheet of words relating to the story, your business, or product. Think of all of the possible variations in spelling and ways people might look for that item or news. Write down the number of searches next to each word or phrase using a keyword tool. Then record the number of competing sites using the allintitle search. Look for a phrase with the balance between high volume and low competition.

I could announce my new book using the title in a press release headline. Or I could do research to figure out how people might be finding this information and use those keywords in the title instead. I picked the keyword phrase "online press releases." So my title could be: "Online Press Releases: Get Traffic and Drive Sales—New Book Explains How." Now I'm using a keyword phrase in the title. If someone links to my book with the title, it's automatically a keyword link.

If you're trying to build a brand or fill the search engines with positive news about your company, your company name might be the main keyword.

Another way to find good keywords or story ideas is to look in your own stats. Look at what words people are using to find your website. Search for terms that are questions, such as "how" or "why." If it doesn't make a good press release, create an article, or blog post on the subject.

If you run paid search engine advertising, use the information from your account to find words that cost a lot per click but result in sales. SpyFu (http://www.spyfu.com) can give you an idea of what advertisers are spending per click on ads. If they are willing to spend $6 on a single click, it's a valuable keyword and it could be for you. It also tells you what unpaid keywords a site ranks well for. Focus on these words or variations of them in your press release.

If you have the expertise or can hire someone to run a paid search campaign, it can provide valuable insightful about what keywords work best for your business. The ads show up when people types words you specify into a search engine.

Finding and Using Keyword Phrases, Step by Step

1. Brainstorm different keywords relating to your news. Think about the problem you solve, the audience you reach, or your brand names.

2. Research the phrases people are typing into search engines using a keyword tool. This can give you new marketing ideas for future press releases and promotions.

3. Compare the volume of searches with the competition.

4. Identify 1–4 different but related keyword phrases to focus on in your press release.

5. Use those keywords and related words in the title of the press release. Use one as anchor text. Use them in the copy of your press release (especially the first sentence, as a link to a related page of your website).

Let's say you sell tickets online and want to come up higher on the list when someone types in "superbowl tickets." You researched it and found there are people searching for this phrase.

Use the most important keyword phrase first. To optimize for the words "superbowl tickets" the title of your press release could be "Price of Superbowl Tickets are Rising Says XYZ.com." Then in the body of the press release you'd link the words "superbowl tickets" to a page of your website, a video, article, or blog post that is about superbowl tickets. Then work in related terms like "price of superbowl tickets" and link to your order page.

Example of using a Keyword Tool for Market Research

Using this example, you can get a quick idea of demand by typing the word TICKETS in freekeywords.wordtracker.com. You'll learn the words people are using to find Superbowl tickets on the Internet.

703	superbowl tickets
6	price of superbowl tickets
5	superbowl tickets contests
4	bid on superbowl tickets
4	superbowl tickets giveaway
3	how to win superbowl tickets
3	need superbowl tickets cheap

The number to the right gives an approximate idea of the number of searches in a given month for that term. It is usually much higher than this (this doesn't include data from Google, the largest search engine).

Keyword research can also give you ideas that you can use in marketing or future press releases.

There are a lot of searches for "superbowl tickets" and over 100,000 other sites about that on Google when I ran this search.

Another benefit of keyword research is to see demand—or the approximate number of Internet searches for a term. Looking at the keyword research you'll see that price is a theme. People want to see the price, win tickets, or find cheap tickets to the Super Bowl.

The first thing I would do after reviewing this information is to craft a press release centering around the price or winning tickets (as above). Then I'd give examples of the rise in prices, why they're high, and even run a contest to help out fans looking for free tickets. You could get creative and say to enter, people have to blog about the game and link back to your website with a keyword phrase as the link text.

Keyword Placement—Prominence and Placement

Identify a keyword phrase or a few keyword phrases to focus on.

Prominence and placement matter and can help you rank higher for those terms.

1. Start by using a keyword phrase in the title of your press release. Sometimes this makes the title too cumbersome, so if it doesn't work focus on being catchy.
2. Use the keyword or a variation on it again in the first sentence or paragraph.
3. Link the keywords to relevant pages or blog posts on your website or a landing page.
4. Use the keyword in various forms in the body of your press release and again, link the words to related web pages. But don't overdo it—no more than once or twice every 100 words.
5. Use the keyword in the last sentence of the press release and make the phrase link to your website.
6. Make the last sentence a call to action or invitation to learn more. For example: ask people to purchase your book, visit your trade-show booth, sign up for your newsletter, enter a contest, or other measureable actions. You might even create a special landing page specific to the news. You can further entice them to take action by putting quotes, success stories, and other elements of persuasion.

Optimize the URL

Increase search engine visibility when possible by optimizing the URL. That means using a keyword in the URL. If you put the news release on your site, try to name the file using keywords. PRWeb lets you put keywords in the URL if you pay at the $200 level or above. It's in the advanced options and is called "URL keywords." You can only choose two words.

Some sites take the title of your press release as the page title automatically. This can be effective as long as the URLs don't become unusually long.

There are two reasons to optimize a URL. First, Google prefers shorter URLs with actual words and not numbers or characters. People tend to click on friendly URLs that are shorter.

Which URL would you rather click on or which would you remember better:

www.yourcompany.com/signup
or
http://www.yourcompany.com/pages/signup/errors/premium/?gid=32dcef5b-896e-4f46-a95f-26c4ed322dba&ReturnUrl=%2longtitle%2f

Since a search engine tries to deliver the most relevant results for a particular search, having a link that people click on increases your credibility, and therefore your ranking.

Use Links

Links are the currency of the Internet. Each site you link to is like a vote for that site. If you get a link from a respected site, it can bolster your own site and its credibility. For example, if CNN wrote a story about the rise of mom entrepreneurs in a recession, and linked to your site, you would gain instant credibility.

One of the biggest mistakes is not putting links in your press release. It limits the distribution of your news if you do not include links.

Use Keywords as Links

Anchor text are words that become links. Rather than clicking on the words www.shoesrus.com, you can use anchor text such as the words: basketball shoes. So when someone clicks "basketball shoes" they go to http://www.shoesRUs.com. The biggest mistake people make is to link only to their home page and only list the URL. In this example the words "basketball shoes" should link to the section of the website specifically about basketball shoes.

7 Distribution—How to Get the Word Out Online

You should post your news on your own website and if you have a blog, write about the news and link to the press release. To be sure your news is seen by more people and gets on more websites, use an online distribution service. These range from free to up to hundreds of dollars and the adage that you get what you pay for usually applies.

Choose a service that has some authority (see PageRank) and can distribute your news to major news sites. There are several free or affordable distribution sites that get you into Google News and Yahoo News, which are the among the largest news portals on the Internet. See the list of worthwhile press release sites in the appendix.

In general, I don't advise using free distribution sites or only using the best quality free sites. Most are low quality. Google doesn't place a lot of trust in most free sites so getting placement or a link from them is practically worthless. Some are even viewed as spam sites and getting a link on the site will only be worthless but it could hurt your credibility with search engines online. The company you keep and the neighborhoods you are a part of online do matter.

Check the PageRank of free sites. Just because they were rated well last year isn't a guarantee of future quality or rankings. Look to be sure the site hasn't been overrun with "make money online" and similar types of "press releases" that have little or no news value. Your website could be devalued by getting links on these types of sites.

PRWeb

I'm a big fan of PRWeb because of the extra features and large distribution they offer for a bargain price. You can get some high quality links this way. Their online reach is similar to much bigger news distribution sites like Businesswire, but the cost is so reasonable and you don't have to purchase packages. For small businesses, it's one of the best options. It takes some time to learn their submission process, but it's worth learning.

In addition to distributing your news release to the top 100 newspapers in the country, PRWeb also distributes to the top online news sources. This includes: Yahoo! News, Google News, Lycos News, Topix.net, Excite News, and eMediaWire.

PRWeb has stats, and 24-hour phone and email support. They are very responsive and helpful. They have daily webinars on how to maximize their service that I highly recommend. Plus you can put money into your account and use it any time.

Most of the time the extra features PRWeb offers (and the editorial staff) are worth the cost. I've seen good distribution at the $80 level but it's basic—you cannot have any links (you can type in the URL but it won't become a link), keywords in the URL, embedded files, or other features.

PRWeb also excels at SEO features. To maximize SEO benefits, choose the $200 distribution. A list of prices is available at: http://www.prweb.com/pr/press-release-price.html.
For most press releases, it's worth the extra cost and it is the least expensive level PRWeb offers that allows anchor text.

PRWeb has the following features built in that make it attractive for SEO:

- In the submission process you enter a list of keywords. The keywords become meta keywords in the code of the site.

- You can specify keyword phrases that you want to become links or "anchor text" in the body of your press release. This is a key SEO feature.

- The title of your press release becomes the title of the web page. (Each web page has a title that search engines use to determine what that page is about. Normally you change the title of a page in the code but PRWeb does this automatically. That title then becomes the clickable link in search results. When you put keywords in the title it helps you rank higher for those words. In fact, this is one of the single most important factors in ranking higher for a keyword or phrase.

- The summary of your news becomes the meta description of the web page. This description is often used by search engines to describe a web page listed in search results. Again, this is usually specified in the code of your site but PRWeb automatically creates it for you using the news summary.

Yahoo News and Google News are some of the largest online news sites on the Internet. Your press release will stay in each of these sites for a total of 28 days.

NOTE: If you edit your press release after it's been distributed it will be excluded in Google News. Currently they have no way to update press releases once they are live on the site. If you have changes, I recommend waiting until after the 28 days before making them.

To get a 5, your news should be well-written, tied into a larger trend, and follow PRWeb guidelines. If you follow what I've recommended in this book, your chances of getting a 5 will increase.

I've seen press releases that have been out a year have fewer impressions and clicks than one that was only out a week. Ideally, if you have a good story and distribute it well (using all of the tools PRWeb offers) those numbers will continue to grow for years. So instead of a year with 34,000 impressions and 1500 clicks, the number is often over 100K impressions and several thousand clicks. One reason it's tough to measure ROI over time, and why this is such a good investment, is that your press release will continue to send people to your site for years after it's released.

If you don't have a newsroom on your site, or a page with all your press and contact information, PRWeb offers an easy solution. However, it's best to put the press releases on your own website because that content will help your search engine rankings. You can also format your press release any way you want to—including adding more links or headings, bold, and italicized text.

PRWeb has daily webinars that are free and excellent. They sometimes give coupon codes for a free press release at the end of their webinar. Sign up for the beginner webinar and, when you feel comfortable with it, try the advanced version.

Social Media Press Releases

Social media press releases are written to attract attention from social media and incorporate sharing and multimedia into the press release. Rather than just text, they come alive with pictures, video and improved formatting. If your story is told best with pictures or is like a good feature story, a social media press release is a good pick. A social media press release is made to be shared on social networking sites.

PRWeb has many elements of a social media press release built in. Another service that I like is Pitch Engine (http://www.pitchengine.com). On Pitch Engine you pay a monthly fee to keep your press release online. While I prefer not to pay monthly I have seen quick results (top search engine rankings within a few days) from the site. Unless you don't mind paying monthly, Pitch Engine is ideal for events or promotions that will expire.

For a premium social media press release there is PRNewsWire's MultiVu. It is the most robust social media press release resource I've seen. It's priced higher and is a good option for larger companies. Find it at http://thedigitalcenter.com.

It's ideal to have a newsroom on your own website to put all your press information and press releases. Then you get the traffic, it's all on your branded domain, and it expands the amount of content on your site, which helps search engine rankings. If you lack the technical resources to create one, Pitch Engine and PRWeb (along with others) will host a newsroom for you for a monthly fee. You could link to the newsroom from your website.

TIP: If you don't have your own newsroom there are services that will host one for you. Just remember that when you stop paying for the newsroom, your press releases will no longer be there. Ideally you should host a social press room on your site. However, that may not be practical for all businesses.

Paid vs. Free Press Release Distribution Websites

If all that matters to you is getting some links to your site and saving money, free press release distribution sites can be valuable tools. I don't recommend free sites but, if you do use them, find ones with good page rank and a permanent link (one that doesn't expire).

Some free sites make you pay to keep the press release on their site after a defined number of days. Also, free sites usually make money by putting ads on your press release. Most look very cluttered and unpro-fessional. Your press release may be distributed to low quality sites, which won't help your visibility very much. Don't expect a help desk or extra features. Most free sites won't allow anchored text or live links in the press release, which to me defeats the purpose.

Experiment with different sites. If you can't put in links, still use keywords and put the URL in the text next to the keywords. Even though people can't click to go there, it gives some association of your site with the keywords.

Last of all, test everything. That's the best way to evaluate sites. A site that is trusted today may be delisted or demoted in search engines tomorrow. Run a press release on different sites. Try different headlines and combinations. See the results and cost and choose what works best for you.

Sometimes a free or lower cost site does the job best and then, for bigger news, you may want to pay more and get the additional features.

How to Evaluate a Press Release Distribution Site:

Free press release sites aren't usually a good value, but if you use them, be sure to evaluate them and choose the best ones. Perhaps the best free PR site is PR.com. I like them because they allow you to create a company profile where you can put keywords. It can serve as a press kit. PR.com also lets you use anchor text in your press releases. You'll get on sites like Yahoo! News, Google News, MSN News and other news sites and you'll get an RSS feed of your press releases.

Sometimes people think that more is better, so they post their press releases on as many sites as possible. I'd choose the best quality sites and test to see what works. In general it's a waste of time to submit to hundreds of free sites.

Here are some questions to consider:

- Do they allow clickable links? Some free sites are text-only. While you can type in a URL it's not clickable.

- Do they allow text (anchor) links? Some sites only allow links with the URL as the text, not words. For SEO value, it's really important to use keyword phrases as link text.

- Can you use keywords in the URL? Click on any press release and see how the URL is structured.

- Look at the time of distribution. Is it same day, next day or 2-day distribution? Some free sites may take up to a week or more to distribute your press release.

- Can you schedule press releases in advance? It is convenient to be able to schedule press releases into the future.

- Do they archive your press releases?

- Can you make edits to a press release after it's live? If you notice a problem with your press release it's unlikely you can fix it and they usually won't allow you to resubmit the same press release twice.

- Look at the quality of press releases on the site. Does an editorial staff approve press releases? If they are spammy or low quality or with garish ads, look elsewhere.

- What is their support like? Usually this isn't important but, when you need to talk to someone, it's good to know someone is there to answer the phone or an email.

- Do you get analytics to see how many times your press release was viewed and other stats?

- Will you get a permanent link in search engines included in the price? Some sites make you pay a monthly fee or your link is gone when you stop paying.

- Do the URLs include keyword phrases? Some like PRWeb let you change the URL to include two keywords, others automatically use all or part of the press release at the end of the URL. Generally speaking you want short URLs because they are easier to share, don't break when they wrap, and are more search engine friendly.

- Is the support by email or phone? Some sites I've used don't answer email quickly and don't have a phone number to contact them.

- Where does the site distribute news? Look for Google News, Yahoo News, Associated Press, MSNBC, and other trusted sites.

- Does the site offer stats about the press release and at what cost?

- Can you embed images, files, or video into your press release? If they allow images, can you use captions? Is that important to you?

Chapter

8 Submitting your Press Release to PRWeb

Every online PR site has its own way of adding links and its unique process for submitting a press release. By far the most comprehensive is PRWeb. They provide statistics so you can see how many people clicked on your press release and how many times the headline was viewed (impressions). This gives you an idea of how your press release is doing in search engines.

You can schedule a press release to go live at a specific day and time. You can also create an account and manage many press releases for multiple clients or accounts in one place. This makes it easy to compare your press releases to see which perform best and use the feedback to help you improve results.

Here are some features of a PRWeb press release:

Pricing

Right now you have three options, starting at $80. All get your news into Google and Yahoo News and allow image and document attachments. The next level up adds social bookmarking to your press release. The $80 level is effective if branding is your primary goal.

I recommend the $200 level release because of the SEO features like anchored text, keyword URLs, and next-day distribution. If you want distribution to the Associated Press and want to embed video, their top level distribution offers that and a lot of extra features.

Distribution Date

At the $200 paymentlevel or above your press release will be distributed the next day. Otherwise it takes two days. The default setting is two days, so change it to be the exact day you want your press release to go live on the site. If you want media coverage, in addition to search engine optimization value, your best chances are during the first part of the week: Monday–Thursday. Test this to see if this matters to your industry.

Headline

Keep your headline to 80 characters or less. Use keyword phrases you want to rank for first. Try to use keywords and capture attention. You can do an informal poll or test headlines. I run the occasional poll on Twitter and it's usually clear which is better. The title will become the link to your press release in search results. And the title is one of the determining factors on how search engines decide what pages are most relevant.

Summary

This is a short description of your press release. It will become an italicized summary of the news under the title and before the main body. Sell your story here in 1–4 sentences. No links or HTML code is allowed but you can use keywords.

Body

This is the main part of your press release. Be sure you spellcheck before you put the press release in the body. Lead with the city, state (PRWEB) and release date. PRWeb formatting will remove bold or italics and formatting such as the font face, bold or italics. If you have bullet points in your press release they will become asterisks.

Use short paragraphs and sentences. Use links. You can put in one link for every 100 words. To make a link first put the full URL starting with http:// and then put the words you want linked in brackets like this example:

> How to Write http://www.happyabout.info [Online Press Releases that Sell]. The words "Online press releases that sell" will become a link to the URL before the words.

Link to related pages on your website, blog posts, your Facebook profile, or supplemental stories on other sites, not just to your home page.

Boilerplate

At the end of every press release put in an About Us or boilerplate section. This is a very brief overview of what your company does and who you are. Include your URL. Then invite people to take action such as purchase your book—and link to the order page.

Quotes

Quotes are important. At the $200 level and up your quote will become a callout (called quoteables) and each quote will be rotated so each time someone accesses your press release, they'll see a different quote. Make your quotes readable and interesting. They should tell a part of the story since it's one of the first things people read. If I only skimmed your quotes, would I want to keep reading? Keep them short or they'll be cut off. Put at least two quotes in your press release.

Keywords

In this box put all of the various keywords that relate to your press release. Use plural versions, abbreviations (state names spelled out and abbreviated), misspellings, and alternate ways people will search for your press release.

Technorati Tags

These are one-word terms that relate to your news. They will be listed below your press release and link to all information tagged with the same word on Technorati. See an example from a press release about a dentist that added a Technorati tag "dentist," http://technorati.com/tag/dentist.

Industry

Depending on the level you pay for you can select industry targets that help focus the distribution of your press release.

Metropolitan Areas or MSA

On PRWeb, journalists sign up for digests or headlines of the news for a particular metropolitan area. Hit major cities across the country unless your press release is a local story. If you want to target a specific place, also mention the name or area in the body of the press release near your keyword phrase.

For example, use Google Insights for Search and type in keywords relating to your news. Find what area shows the most interest. If your news is international, research which countries to focus on. For example, "Sydney, Australia, PR firm" would increase your chances.

Contact Info

PRWeb asks for contact info for the person responsible for answering inquiries about your news. Include the media contact's name, company name, email, country, zip code, and phone number.

RSS Feeds

PRWeb allows you to create an RSS feed of your news that you can add to your website or blog. Name the RSS feed with your company name and a keyword phrase. When you group your press releases this way they will automatically show a list of links to your previous press releases below each press release.

Pictures or Media Attachments

Studies have shown that people are drawn to the caption under a photo. Many people don't include a caption or put the company's name as a caption. Instead, put a 'call to action' or summarize one of the most interesting facts of your story under the picture. If you don't have a good photo, put your company logo.

SEO TIP: Put a keyword phrase in the file name of your image and in the description.

PRWeb is one of the few distribution sites that allows a caption under images and photos. At the highest level you can also embed a video into your press release. These can be very effective as studies have shown that top bloggers link more often to video (or put video on their blog posts) than to any other content.

URL Keywords

Keywords are words that people type into search engines that relate to your business. Most often it's a phrase or a question, such as "Where can I buy fashion sunglasses?" If you sell sunglasses, the word "fashion sunglasses" might be an important keyword phrase.

As part of search engine optimization and at the PRWeb $200 level you can specify two keywords that will become part of your press release URL. This is in the advanced section. Choose the most important words that related to your story. Once you choose the words, you cannot change them for any reason. If you misspell a word, or after your news is approved, it's too late.

SEO Wizard

I've found this to be practically useless except to give you an idea of word density. It doesn't focus on phrases but single words. Single words are far too competitive.

Preview

Use this to see how your press release will look with the links, images, and everything. Whatever URL you put for your company, it will show up in a preview pane under your press release. So make it go to a relevant page—again, it might not be your home page.

At the bottom of each press release there is a trackback URL, a place for readers to add their comments, social bookmarking sites, and links to other press releases by the same company.

Here are the social bookmarking sites that are listed at the bottom of each press release:

Del.icious, Furl, Technorati, Ask, MyWeb, Propeller, Live Bookmarks, Newsvine, TailRank, Reddit, Slashdot, Digg, SumbleUpon, Google Bookmarks, Sphere, Blink It, Spurl.

You can increase your news visibility by bookmarking your press release. I also suggest making a blog post in informal writing (perhaps with more screenshots and details), linking to your press release, and bookmarking the post.

PRWeb gives basic stats about your press release. Here is what they say (from PRWeb):

Reads - This number tells you how many times your press release was accessed from our site and other distribution points where we have the ability to measure a click through. This number does not include the number of journalists that have received your release through email. In addition there are online distribution points that we currently have no ability to track.

Estimated Pickup - This number estimates the number of times your press release was picked up by a media outlet. This does not tell you how many times your story appears in the media. It simply attempts to estimate media interest of your release.

Prints - This is the number of times that someone has printed your press release. We measure this by the number of times that the "printer friendly version" link is pressed. In reality, only a small percentage of users actually click this link before printing a release.

Forwards - This is the number of times that someone has forwarded your press release to a third party using the link on your press release.

PDF Downloads - The number of times your release was downloaded as a PDF document. PDF Downloads may be reflected in "Reads" and "Estimated Pickup" statistics.

Here are some comparisons between some of the top press release distribution sites:

Service	Price	Features
PRWeb	No membership fee. Lowest cost is $80 and the SEO Visibility option is $200. To add video is $360.[1] Also distributes to Business Wire.[2]	"Gets picked up in leading online news sites like Yahoo! News, Google News, Ask.com, and Topix. Additionally, your press release is distributed through a host of other online news sites including our own PRWeb.com and eMediaWire.com, which deliver over 50 million page views each month."

Service	Price	Features
PRNewswire	The standard news release that runs about 400 words can be sent to all media in your state, plus trade publications, and also distributed to more than 5,000 websites, online services and databases for as little at $180 for a locally targeted press release.[3]	"Your message will reach mainstream and industry trade media, thousands of web outlets and PR Newswire for Journalists, a digital media channel serving more than 85,000 registered journalists across the globe." Distributed to more than 5,000 websites, databases and online services, such as Yahoo, MSN, and AOL.
Business Wire	Around $200 for a local story.	Your full-text press release is delivered to thousands of online outlets directly and through news syndicates. Your news appears on major news sites including BusinessWire.com, Yahoo!, Google News, and AOL; and is archived at all major databases including Factiva and Lexis/Nexis.[4]

Service	Price	Features
Market Wire	Contact the company directly to get a quote but prices for US distribution is around $499. Charges $75 for anchor text. Has SEO/Online features.	See list of distribution points.[5]
24-7pressrelease.com	Statistics available at $49 includes cost per display and cost per view. Can attach files, logos or images to press release. Distribution through RSS and JavaScript feed subscribers. For $89 you can add video. $349 gets distribution to PR Newswire media only website accessed by 80,000 journalists, distribution to 4000+ websites and trade publications for your industry.[6]	Reaches nearly 80,000 journalists, 4000+ websites including PR Newswire, Yahoo News, Google News, CBS Market watch, MSNBC, ABC News, CNN.com, AOL, and more. $40 option for SEO. It does allow anchored links (unlimited) and has a staff that takes calls during business hours. The basic package for $49 offers great SEO benefits. They also allow formatting such as bold, italics, underline, etc. They offer next day distribution and scheduling for paid packages.

Service	Price	Features
eReleases.com	$399 includes an online newsroom and submits to PRNewswire.[7]	Goes to over 40,000 journalists, to national newspapers, radio and television stations, along with SEO and social media sharing features.

1. See http://www.prweb.com/pr/press-release-price.html for current pricing and features
2. See http://www.prwebdirect.com/catalog.php for pricing
3. http://services.prnewswire.com/SmallBusiness/PRN_SB_Pricing.pdf
4. http://bit.ly/businesswire
5. http://www.marketwire.com/mw/include.do?module=DIST&pageid=486
6. http://www.24-7pressrelease.com/pricing_plans.php
7. http://www.ereleases.com/submit.html

9 Assembling PR Contacts in your Industry

You've sent out a press release and now you're waiting for the results. I wish I could tell you that your job is done. But it's not—to get better coverage you need to also build relationships with PR contacts. These relationships can bring you valuable links and get you onto highly trafficked websites or blogs.

Create a List of Contacts and follow them or list where the URLs of their profiles on Social Sites (Twitter, Facebook, Delicious, etc). Do this for bloggers and Mainstream Media.

You should identify influential people in your industry and keep notes about what they cover. For example, About.com guides cover various topics online and have a lot of credibility. You can form relationships with them and possibly be a source or get a link if you have relevant news.

Here are some free websites where you can find journalists or media outlets both in the US and internationally:

Media Post (http://www.mediapost.com/)
Directory to over 100,000 media, marketing and advertising professionals.

NewsLink.org (http://newslink.org)
Directory of newspapers and media outlets by state and tells you which
are the most linked to media outlets.

ABYZ News Links (http://www.abyznewslinks.com/)
Directory for media contacts in different countries

Contacting Journalists

In addition to distributing a press release, you'll also want to let journalists who write about the topic of your press release know about your story. Most journalists prefer email. While they will listen to voicemail, they rarely return calls unless your pitch is compelling and on-topic for what they're writing about. If they have your phone number and need information, they'll call you. Calling to make sure they got the press release is annoying—don't do it.

If you bother people, you'll get blacklisted and ruin your reputation with them. Calling to see if you can offer any help or to see if they're likely to run a story is better. However, email is best.

Be brief; try to think what might be interesting to them. If you don't hear back, they're probably not interested. Don't mass blast to a large group. Instead contact one person at a time and change your pitch to match what they write about.

Get straight to the point and link to the full story. Always put it in the light of "what's in it for you" or why they might be interested. Research what the person you're sending the pitch to writes about and tailor your message to that.

Here are some general guidelines in writing an email to a journalist:

1. Write a short and descriptive subject line.
2. Keep it short. Get to the point quickly. If possible tie it into something they've written about recently.
3. Include a few sentences, a few facts, and why they're important/relevant. Bullet points are great.

4. Provide one or two helpful links, including one to the press release.

5. Leave contact information and a note of your expertise in case you could be a source for a future story.

Make sure the story is relevant to what the writer covers. Don't send a pitch about your new software to a writer who covers parenting (unless the software is for parents specifically).

Use HARO for Story Ideas

Rather than guessing what stories journalists and bloggers are interested in, HARO has actual requests for information. It's a good way to get ideas and to see who covers what. Start tracking who writes about topics that relate to your business. You can't email them with other pitches besides specifically what they ask for. Remember not to ruin your reputation and go against HARO rules by sending unsolicited email.

Media on Twitter

Here is a very helpful way to find reporters, news outlets, and bloggers on Twitter. http://mediaontwitter.pbwiki.com/US+-+Media+on+Twitter, Media on Twitter breaks down the contacts by state and has an international section for outside of the US.

TIP: JibberJobber (http://www.jibberjobber.com) is a great CRM (contact relationship manager) that can help you keep track of all of your contacts and notes. A basic account is free.

Write About Your News on Your Own Blog

Summarize the news and make it more personal. Go over the main points. Add additional information. Then use a keyword phrase to link to the actual press release. Sites like Digg won't link directly to a press release on a news site, but you can submit a blog post. Also, bloggers usually prefer to link to another blog post rather than a press release.

PRLeap has a great way that you can embed a press release on your blog or web page. You insert code and your news will appear in a Flash viewer. That way you can still link to the full press release but anyone can also read it right on your blog.

TIP: If you do not have a company blog, create a free blog at Fast Company. To get started, go to http://www.fastcompany.com and sign up for an account. Fast Company ranks well and you can get the information up quickly while waiting for your own blog or if you don't have enough content to start a separate blog of your own.

How to Find Top Blogs

Alltop - http://www.alltop.com is a blog aggregator that chooses the top blogs in different niches. It's a great place to find influential bloggers who might be interested in writing about your news.

Check newspaper sites or magazine sites which often have blogs written by journalists. These often have high authority and trust so getting a link on an industry blog can really help spread your news.

Technorati - http://www.technorati.com is a blog search engine that ranks the popularity of blogs. You can find specific blog posts about a subject or entire blogs about a subject.

Google Blog search - http://blogsearch.google.com is another way to find bloggers who write in your area of interest.

http://www.google.com/reader is a tool to help you subscribe online to the blogs that are writing good content. This is like subscribing to a magazine or newspaper. Instead of having to go and buy each new issue when it comes out, they send it or deliver it directly to you. RSS readers or blog readers do the same by letting you know when bloggers have updated their blog. You don't have to go to their blog to see if there's something new, the blog reader lets you know. You can see many recent posts from all the blogs you're tracking in one place.

How to Find People on Twitter with Influence

The site http://www.Twitterholic.com lists top people on Twitter with the number of people they follow and the number of people who follow them. You can click on a city or state name and get the top people by geographic location. There are also online Twitter directories like http://www.Twellow.com that identify people on Twitter by topic.

Social Bookmarking

Social bookmarking your news increases exposure of your press release or blog post. These are sites that take votes for stories. There are many. Some of the top sites are:

Digg (http://www.digg.com) covers mainly technical/science type of stories which you can submit and other people can vote and comment on the story. People can join your network and keep up with your newest submissions.

Delicious (http://delicious.com) is an online bookmarking site. Rather than saving your favorite websites to your personal computer, you save and share them online. You can download icons for your browser and can easily save any web page you come across. You can also create notes about the page, and add tags. You can also get your own URL so others can see what you've bookmarked. I have created an account at http://www.newspapergrl.com/online-pr. I constantly add new websites that are about online PR, and saving them on Delicious makes it easy to share them.

Delicious is also social in that you can see how many other people have bookmarked a web page and the tags they used. Top sites get promoted to the home page.

StumbledUpon (http://www.stumbleupon.com) - Submit a site and users give sites a thumbs up or thumbs down. People can join your network. The more people vote on your site the higher it rises. It can be an effective way to get traffic to a new website or other pages of your site. You can also pay to be featured.

Kirtsy (http://www.kirtsy.com) - Similar to Digg but for relationship and lifestyle types of stories. Some call it the Digg for women.

There are many social sites that fill different niches. These are some of my favorites but you can experiment to see what works best for you. Ask your staff to sign up for and learn each of these sites. Whenever you have news you can ask them to bookmark it.

Automate posting on social sites with Social Poster:
http://www.socialposter.com. I like **Social Poster** because it's free and gives a quality link back to your site and has high PageRank. Fill out your site information (or post info) and choose the sites you want to submit to. Choose the frame version and you'll get a toolbar above each login page. When you finish submitting to one you click "next" and register or submit to the next site. They have about 160 different social bookmarking sites to choose from. Just getting to the right 'sign on page' saves time and hassle.

10 Not One Press Release, a Campaign

The secret shortcut of online promotion...is that there is no secret shortcut. Step by step, bit by bit, link by link, you build something important and powerful.
Seth Godin, Marketing Expert and Author

One of the biggest mistakes I see companies make is that they often release one press release and call it good. Or they release news very sporadically. If you stop talking people forget about you. Keeping the conversation going is good marketing and press releases are a way to keep talking, being found, and being heard. Google rewards consistency (it's a way to build authority and trust in search engines), so try to plan a regular schedule of news every month or every few months.

When you consistently release information about your company, you are rewarded by search engines. Consistency is a way of building trust online. Think about it in terms of a relationship—if you don't know someone but expect them to buy something from you the first time you introduce yourself to them, then you will be disappointed. But if they get used to seeing your name and your message resonates with them, they may begin to trust you. That's the first step to building a relationship. Over time that relationship can lead to sales. That's very different from an advertising model where the entire intention is selling.

Let me illustrate with actual statistics. One of my clients issued their first press release at the beginning of 2008. I looked at the stats for June 2009 and the press release has 91046 impressions and 2284 clicks. Their most recent press release has only been out a month but it already has 264808 impressions and 2595 clicks. After a year this number will increase dramatically.

At first they didn't see much impact but sometime during the first several months the phones started to ring. Customer service didn't know that marketing was sending out press releases but suddenly they were getting leads. Since then the company has released news each month. There is always variation in your stats depending on the appeal of the topic and the headline, but consistent effort pays off.

Most businesses need to send out regular press releases before deciding if the investment is worth it. The biggest complaint I hear is that a press release didn't get any results, but most likely they only sent one or two a year. Compared to the price of advertising it's really a bargain and, as I've pointed out earlier, sending out press releases can't be the only marketing you do. It's part of the mix of marketing activities you need to do to promote your business.

Be sure to plan to release news on a regular schedule—but with one caveat—only if you have actual news. Don't make up news or send different variants of the same news. While it's alright to tell different perspectives in newsletters, articles, blog posts and other ways don't keep sending out the same news in a new press release. I've seen clients who send out a press release weekly and the only difference was that it had new stats. If your weekly stats are interesting (not just numbers) then that strategy will work but for most businesses it won't. You will see diminishing returns on your investment. Don't send out weekly press releases just to keep your name out there. Depending on your business, one press release a month is usually enough.

Brainstorm ideas on what is coming up and what you're company is doing. Get in the habit of looking for data or things happening in your business that you can publicize. Plan out a series of press releases around keywords or stories coming up.

Look for the stories in your business. They are everywhere. Then tell them well and optimize them. Adding a human element to your news will build up the human side to your business. It will make it more likely that people know about and trust you.

Regularly communicate through press releases—it's a vital part of your sales and marketing strategy. Using the tips and techniques in this book you'll be a PR ninja online.

Online PR—An Opportunity for PR Firms

PR firms are expected to know more about online PR than they often do. This book is a guide that represents an opportunity to offer clients more expertise. Combined with traditional PR, this adds additional services that PR firms can offer their clients.

E-consultancy surveyed 300 marketers and PR pros in the UK for their Online PR Industry Benchmarking Report. For those who work in companies rather than in an agencies, 39% of PR activity is online. Agencies report that a bit more—47% of their clients' retained fees—come from online PR.

51% of companies use PR agencies to do online PR, 29% use a search marketing agency, and 22% use a web development agency to develop and deliver online PR strategy.

The satisfaction of clients with their PR firm's online PR knowledge and offering vary.

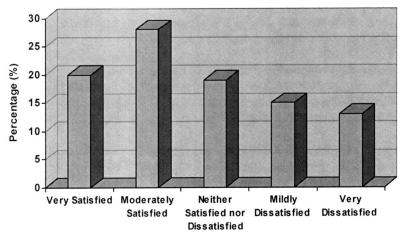

Clients' Satisfaction Rating

PR Firm's Online PR Knowledge—Satisfaction Ratings

Obviously there is a lot of demand for PR firms who can deliver on social media and online PR.

In my experience many of the firms who say that online PR isn't effective aren't doing SEO properly or maximizing what you can do with online press releases. Their results are often only for branding—in other words, reaching people who already know a brand name and search for it. I'd rather get people who are looking for help with a problem that my company can solve. In other words, targeting phrases that people search for.

Another issue is that PR firms often target one word links that are so competitive that they have little hope of ranking for that phrase.

If you need help creating contact listsfind a PR firm that understands online marketing and has experience with social media. To help, here's a study that rates PR firms:
http://blogs.zdnet.com/feeds/?p=512&page=4

Extend the Reach of your News

1. Email key bloggers and journalists first before the news goes to the public. Let them know when it will go live.
2. Once your press release is live, social bookmark your press release and send it to your other contacts.
3. Link to the press release on your website or republish it in your news section.
4. Blog about your press release and track back to it. Social bookmark the post.
5. Add your press release to Facebook, and add your RSS feed to other profile pages (such as Hubspot— http://www.hubspot.com or Squidoo— http://www.squidoo.com).
6. Twitter about your news with a link. You can use this free service http://bit.ly and enter a long URL and get a shorter one. Also, customize your URL with a word relating to the news. Bit.ly also gives analytics so you can tell how many people clicked on the link and it has an archive of every URL you've posted online.
7. Track your news and respond to people who write about it by featuring their replies in tweets or blog posts. Thank them for writing, tweeting, or sharing your news.
8. Ask a question in your press release or blog post about your news. You might ask, " What other features do you want to see in our product?"
9. Include a link to your press release in your newsletter.

HARO Entry

A HARO email starts with categories, and then gives specifics. Here's an example of a part of one email that goes out three times a day. They include pitches from both small and large companies. Some reveal their identities and some don't. Be sure not to respond unless you can offer what they ask by the time requested. Stay on point, leave contact info, and offer to answer more questions if needed.

This resource is fairly new and will continue to evolve. It's a great free service that makes it even easier to get free PR.

To join the list, go to http://www.HelpAReporter.com.

Choosing a Newswire, Questions to Ask

What features you need depends on your business. For SEO purposes that distinguish a regular press release from an online press release, there are some necessary features. Those include links, anchor text links, a permanent link, and an SEO-friendly URL structure. It's also important to note the quality of the site—some are more trusted by search engines than others.

PageRank is an indicator of the authority of a website. Though it's not a perfect one, it can give you an idea of the importance assigned to the particular website. It is a rank of 0–12 but almost no one gets a 12. Getting 4 or above is very good. At first your own press release won't have any PageRank and so after it drops off the home page, it won't provide much value. However, over time and by linking to it on your social media profiles and blog, and as your news gets written about and linked to by others, it can gain importance.

Links

Each site has their own convention on how to add links. Most charge more for the capability. To make words into links or anchored text as it's called, you might need to know how to do a little basic coding in HTML.

<a href=http://www.newspapergrl.com>www.newspapergrl.com</a> will look like www.newspapergrl.com.

To make words into a link, use words instead of a URL (notice there are no spaces by the brackets):

<a href=http://www.newspapergrl.com>Newspapergrl online market-er</a> will look like Newspapergrl online marketer.

Some sites have their own way of creating link. PRWeb has you put the full URL first and then the words you want as links following the URL, in brackets:

http://www.massageregister.com/MassageTherapySchools/Massage-TherapySchools.asp?State=WA-Washington   [massage   therapy   schools in Washington]

When published the reader only sees this:
MassageTherapy Schools in Utah.

11 Promoting your News

There's a lot that you can do to promote your news after it's released.

Contact Bloggers

Journalists read blogs for story ideas and blogs often rank well in search engines. Some blogs have powerful pull with their readers or a community of people who read their blog. A link on a well-ranked blog can be more valuable than any other sources of links.

There are two types of bloggers—individual bloggers and bloggers who are part of the media who blog for their publications. If you email a regular blogger, remember that a commercial pitch will probably turn them off. You'll need to take a more laid back, personal approach.

Bloggers often have big egos (I know because I am one), so be sure to keep that in mind. Show that you've taken time to see what they write about and their interests. Some sites like Marketing Pilgrim (http://www.MarketingPilgrim.com) are more friendly to getting press releases (as long as it's about Internet marketing) or news. Others are less so.

Individual bloggers often want to know that you understand their niche and make your pitch relevant to them and their readers. You can start building a relationship by first knowing what they write about. Then you can comment on their blog or reach out to them on Twitter. You may also find bloggers who've already written about you or your competitors. They might already be evangelists of your company. Develop a relationship with them and let them know about new things happening in your business. Email them stories first and let them be "in the know."

Most bloggers have a contact form, which is my favorite way to contact them. Other bloggers make it tough to find out how to contact them. Some simply type their email address somewhere in the sidebar like this:

Janet [at] affiliateflash [dot] com

Remember you don't have a lot of control over what a blogger writes. They will give their own opinion and link to whatever they want. They may not write what you hoped (a glowing report), but it can get you exposure to their audience. Plus, it's a chance to start a dialog with them or with their audience. If they do write about you, jump on and comment on the post. Post follow-up comments to clarify or add to the discussion.

If someone writes something negative, respond to them as quickly as possible. Acknowledge what they've said and let them know you noticed and are paying attention (that you care). Correct any errors. Offer to make changes if you can. Lend your expertise and help should they want to contact you directly about the issue. If possible, call them and discuss the issue. It's much easier to deal with negative reviews in the beginning than to wait until it's snowballed into something bigger.

Just remember a blogger isn't a paid representative and doesn't necessarily have to go by the rules in the business world. Some are anti-corporate. They tend to be opinionated and have a distinct style or tone. Some may get offended easily. I cannot stress enough to be sure you understand their likes and dislikes before approaching them. Spend time reading their blog and be sure it's a good fit. Keep in mind that quality is better than mass. If you read that Kraft foods is flying them out to sample the newest program or they just made a television show they might not be interested in a $10 product sample. So make it worth their effort.

Google routinely sends email to bloggers asking if they saw a piece of news and offering more information on their blog. Then they leave contact information and links with more information.

Bloggers usually don't get paid for their work (and this topic is controversial). If your product or service fits the topic of their blog ask them if you can send them product samples or give them a free account. Answer their questions or provide tips for their readers. Offer to give them offers or products to give away to their readers. Just know that it's bad form to expect them to return the product and that you've got to make it worth their time.

Guest Posts

Another approach—and bloggers may suggest it especially if you have a blog—is to offer to write a guest post on their blog. That way they have content and they don't need to write. However, they'll only go for this if you show them the post will be helpful to their readers and not a sales pitch or overtly marketing to them.

I was recently contacted by someone who represented an author. Her book fit my audience. She gave me background on the book and offered to send me a free copy to review. Then she offered to provide interviews, videos or other information that might be helpful. It was a good fit for my readers—and I'll write about the book.

Leave Comments

Another way to get bloggers' attention is to participate on their blog. They notice the people who regularly contribute and become part of the community. Leave comments or feature their posts on your blog and link to them.

Email a blogger directly and request a write-up. PR Squared has many excellent examples of email pitches on their blog at http://tinyurl.com/avtj56. Use their ideas to generate your own email pitches.

Ask Someone to Tweet about your News

Many bloggers with a large following are also on Twitter. If they pass along your story on Twitter, it can mean getting thousands of visitors based on their recommendation alone. I suggest you send them a blog post about your news rather than the press release itself. Just email or tweet them asking if they've seen your story and ask them if they'll consider tweeting about it.

Find the contact information on a blog and send them your news. Just make sure your news is relevant. If they never respond or write about your news, it's probably not a good fit.

Google's marketing department routinely sends email to bloggers who write about tech marketing asking if they saw a piece of news and offering more information with a link to a relevant blog post. Then they leave contact information for someone at Google who can answer questions about the news.

Bloggers love to link to video. So if you have video, post it on YouTube and embed it into your press release. Or, just send the link and let the blogger grab it for their blog if they want to.

Write about your News on your Own Company Blog and on Social Networks

Be sure to write a short blurb with the main news points and link to the full press release on your company blog. Make sure to link to the press release using keywords. Tweet about the news and add it to various social networks you're a part of linking to the blog post not the press release. Sites like Digg do not allow press releases and people on social networks are usually more open to reading or linking to a blog post than getting a link to a press release.

Here are my rules for press releases:

1. Don't be boring! If no one is listening—it's probably because you're boring! Here's a great blog post on how to be more interesting: http://tinyurl.com/oklzb5.

2. Keep the story simple and straightforward. Don't use a lot of jargon or industry buzzwords. Make your press release inviting and accessible to anyone, even if they aren't familiar with your industry or business. Don't make someone think too hard to get it.

3. Put the most important information first and get to the main points quickly: the Who, What, When, Where, How and Why.

4. Reiterate or personalize the story with interesting quotes. Quotes should mean something and should make people want to read more. There is nothing I hate more than boring quotes that don't mean anything. I've read so many press releases that say, "We're excited about our new...." Why are you excited? How does your story help people? That's more compelling.

5. Keep ego out of it. Sometimes companies overdo it by putting their name above the story or see a press release as a way to brag or prove themselves. Especially in their boilerplates (the 'About Us' section at the end) they find many variations of saying they are first, number one, the best, etc. That makes people suspicious. Instead, give stats, a brief success story, or results or a survey that is complimentary.

6. People care more about the human element than they care about a particular company. If they care they will find out who you are and they'll remember you.

Elements of a Successful Press Release

- A strong headline that makes people want to keep reading and incorporates keywords.

- An interesting story that helps people connect with and/or trust your company.

- At least two quotes that help illustrate the main points or interesting details of the press release.

- Two to four links to different pages of your website. Be sure you link to a specific page on your site that is related to what you're talking about—not to just the home page.

- A strong call to action at the end with a keyword phrase linking to a landing page specifically related to what your press release is about.

- A good picture that tells the story, with a strong caption underneath.

- A phone number and URL to your site to get more information.

- A media contact who knows about the news and is ready to take inquiries and can answer them quickly.

As important as getting your news out to a wide audience, it's most important to establish yourself as a trusted, credible source of information related to your business. If you don't have a lot of visibility, the tactics in this book will help.

12 Using Social Media for an Online PR Campaign

Social media can create amazing results for far less investment than traditional advertising. They usually have a much longer-lasting effect because they are online even after the campaign is over.

Rather than trying to create your own community, it's usually better to join existing communities. It takes a lot of time to gain a new following. When you work within an existing network you take advantage of the traffic and exposure they have built.

Social media is powerful because of the "word of mouth" aspect. Where you once reached a few people you can reach many more with social media. Social sites make it easy for people to share information with others.

I favor blending traditional and online PR together to expand the reach of your PR campaigns.

Remember the point of belonging to a social network is to be social. So choose where to focus and keep the content updated and fresh.

Here are some of the biggest sites and ways you can use them. Start out with one or two and use different media depending on your audience and goals. Don't feel like you need to use all of them. You can get overwhelmed quickly. Set up profiles and then become active on the site that works best for you.

Facebook

http://www.facebook.com - A general site for sharing information with its own applications, groups, email, and advertising network. You can set it up so it automatically updates with your latest blog posts and press releases.

Talk about how this is growing.

Facebook is a place where people not only share news about their lives but they also go to share their reactions to and feedback about news. When pop icon Michael Jackson died his fans all over the world expressed their dismay and opinions on Facebook and other social sites.

I would write more about Facebook, but Joan Stewart, "The Publicity Hound," has a learning tool that explains it all so well. I recommend it to anyone who wants to learn more about building a presence on Facebook. She has screen captures and detailed information that spells it out for the novice or intermediate Facebook user. Find it here: http://bit.ly/9He2s.

If you use PRWeb you can get an RSS feed of all of your press releases. Email or call them if you need help locating the correct URL to your feed.

Make posts to your wall to keep people informed about what you're doing. Document where your news was picked up (i.e. "we were just covered by Entrepreneur magazine! Link to the story). Try to keep it fun by running contests for those who leave feedback or offering exclusive information or access to your company. The key point on Facebook is to keep it fun.

1. Start a Profile and find fans. When they become a fan it posts to their profile letting all of their friends on Facebook know about you.

2. Find and join relevant groups on Facebook. There are groups for all kinds of interests. Some have thousands of members; others only have a few. You may even want to start a group. You can create a profile for your business and a group for a segment that appeals to Facebook demographics. Groups are ideal for event marketing.

3. Plug in blog posts and press release RSS feeds (if you use PRWeb you can set up an RSS feed of all the news released through their service) using the "notes" feature.

4. Write on people's walls and respond to comments on your page. Send info to your groups.

5. Post photos or videos to your Facebook Page.

6. Learn to use the list feature to send updates just to relevant groups.

Twitter

http://www.twitter.com - I call Twitter your personal PR channel. Or the silent newsroom. It's a great way to bring attention to your story.

Twitter is a microblog—each time you post a short update it goes out to all of your "followers."

It's easy to set up a Twitter profile. Though your updates (or tweets) are not weighted heavily as a link in search engines, tweets are indexed and can show up in web searches.

Each tweet has a unique URL which you can link to. Find it at the bottom of a tweet where it gives the time the message was left. Right click on your mouse to "save URL."

Twitter allows you to write short updates in 140 words or less. You can also send links. People can follow you—or get your updates and you can get theirs. Updates can be sent and read online, through text message, or IM.

You can participate in a discussion of a specific event or topic even if you're not following others in the discussion and they aren't following you. Group discussions are identified by a hash tag (put a pound sign in front of a term—like #apple if discussing apple computer) or a phrase or term relating to the discussion. The most popular terms are called trending terms and display on the right side of your Twitter page. A website called http://www.whatthetrend.com is a search engine of trending topics. You can get an explanation of why a topic is trending on Twitter.

Use this information to quickly identify trends relating to your industry or to flesh out news stories and find sources or stories to support your points.

If you're on Twitter, send out a blurb about your news and link to the press release or blog post about it. Or, find someone in your industry who has a lot of followers and writes about the topic. See if they'll tweet about it. The best way to ask them is with a DM or direct message—but they must be one of your followers to get it. If they don't follow you, try emailing the request. Give them a sample of a tweet to go from and make it faster and easier. I'm much more open to tweeting something if it fits my audience and they give me a great headline and short link.

Paul Wilson (http://www.mymarketer.net) learned the power of Twitter. He left a comment on a post on popular blogger Darren Rowse's blog (http://www.problogger.com) sharing a blog post he created. Darren decided to mention the post to his followers on Twitter. The next day Paul had over 3,000 new visitors to his blog. Following that he had over 4,000 new visitors. This one mention continued to send him new visitors for weeks.

Here's an example of a Twitter update that has a news announcement:

Facebook's Real-Time Homepage Goes Live Today
http://snipurl.com/dma5z

This is a tweet for a Mother's Day campaign for a local jeweler. Notice it's not linking to the press release but to the actual coupon. The organizer of this PR campaign gave bloggers sample posts with URLs to make it easy for them. Here are the examples:

Sample Tweet

Live in UT? Get FREE pearl necklace 4 Mom's Day http://twitpic.com/4crp1 Must redeem @ Goldsmith Jewelers in Provo by 5/9 ($99 value) PLS RT

Sample Facebook Message

Utah folks: Awesome offer! Get a FREE pearl necklace for Mother's Day. Must redeem at the Goldsmith Jewelers store in Provo by 5/9 ($99 value).

NOTE: Upload the image of the coupon link under the message you write.

There are always new tools coming out to help you capitalize on the power of Twitter. Start here:

1. Set up a profile and brand it. I think it's worth it to hire someone to create a custom background with your branding. The Monterey Aquarium is a great example of using a custom Twitter background: http://twitter.com/MontereyAq

2. Use http://wefollow.com to find people to follow, also see if the bloggers you identify are on Twitter and follow them. Then use a service to schedule out posts (before, during, and after a promotion or PR event).

3. Use http://Search.twitter.com to get real time search results and see what people are saying about you. You can save searches so you can track them in real time. Answer people's questions and see who the big players are by using this invaluable tool. The advanced search features let you search by geographical location, which is great for local businesses.

4. If you are posting on Twitter, add pictures with http://twitpic.com. The free service will let you upload an image, give you a URL, and track how many people accessed the image.

5. There are many Twitter services like http://www.TweetDeck.com to help you manage your Tweets. On Tweetdeck you can update Facebook at the same time you update Twitter. It also lets you quickly see who has written to you publicly and privately. Be sure to respond quickly to messages left or tweets about you or your business.

6. Schedule out tweets for publicity. Using a service like http://www.SocialToo.com or http://www.socialoomph.com you can schedule a series of tweets in advance. You can choose the exact time and day your tweet goes live.

7. Use a free tool like http://www.TwitIQ.com to manage more than one Twitter account using a dropdown menu in the upper right hand corner of the site.

Twitter Resources:

Learn about how big brands are using Twitter:
http://mashable.com/2009/01/21/best-twitter-brands/

Top Twitter tools: http://tinyurl.com/c6pc2h

Here's an example of a Twitter Contest run by Overstock.com:
http://tinyurl.com/nkcnwl

To Reach Professionals and Other Businesses—Set up a LinkedIn Profile

http://www.LinkedIn.com - A social network for professionals. Post work experiences, join groups, ask questions, and get recommendations from other professionals. LinkedIn is a good place to conduct polls, find experts for advice or interviews for your stories about workplace or professional issues.

You can do everything from sending out a weekly newsletter to joining and creating groups on LinkedIn. LinkedIn Answers is a valuable tool for business because they reward people for contributing and giving quality answers.

NOTE: For a more in-depth description on using Linked, see 'I'm on LinkedIn—Now What???' by Jason Alba.

---

1. See if there is a company profile on your business. If not, create one.
2. Set up a profile for everyone in your company.
3. On your profile, link to your blog and website with keywords. The default says "My website" and "My blog" but you can change it to say "Online PR blog" etc. You can vary the keywords you use on each profile you create.
4. Change your URL from a generic to a specific one so it looks like this: www.linkedin.com/in/yourbusinessname.
5. Ask questions or join groups to participate. Post professional events (conferences, etc).

To Share Images and Video—Set up a Flickr Account

Flickr is a social site for images and video. You can load images and video and tag them. People can comment and easily share the images. It's a great place to store your digital assets for press releases or to send bloggers to when they write a post about you.

Any time you have an event you should take pictures and create video. It's so easy to do. Assign someone to do this so it happens. Then post the pictures to Flickr where people can comment on them. Be sure to add the video and pictures to your Facebook Profile too.

1. You can get a pro account so you can set up a profile and put all your pictures there. Then you can customize the URL and add branding elements like your logo. Add keyword links back to your site and/or blog on your profile.

2. Get a plugin or Flickr widget that you get from their site can display a slideshow of your pictures (or check out NextGen Wordpress plugin)

For Video—Set up a YouTube Channel

With an inexpensive video camera like the Flip Mino you can easily take video and post it to YouTube. You can then share the video on your blog, Facebook and other social media sites you're active on.

For Bookmarking—Set up a Delicious Account

Delicious is a social bookmarking site for sharing websites. Rather than saving your favorite websites just on your computer, you can save them online and share them with others.

Best of all you can create URLs for each topic so you can reference them in your press or in email. You can add a custom title, notes, and tags for each bookmark. Here's my Delicious URL for the best online PR sites I've found: http://www.delicicous.com/newspapergrl/online_pr. I will update this regularly so be sure to keep checking back (or subscribe to the RSS feed).

Set up an account on Delicious, install the plugins and then bookmark interesting stories you find or blog posts that you want to save.

Niche Social Networks

Each of these social networking sites is general and reaches a large audience except LinkedIn.com, which is specifically for professionals. There are also hundreds of niche social networks to match just about any interest. http://www.newspapergrl.com/2009/02/niche-social-networks/ has a list of many.

Other Social Sites

StumbleUpon - This is another bookmarking site. Give websites (including press releases) a thumbs up or thumbs down and see what sites others like. This site can drive a lot of traffic to your website.

Social Media Case Studies:

I collect social media case studies. While some of these campaigns may be too expensive for a small business, they each have elements that you can use for next to nothing.

Yoplait Yogurt Contest - A great example of using social media to drum up interest in a new product.

http://tinyurl.com/q8vo73

An entrepreneur creates his own PR campaign for his website (not really free, but a "do-it-yourself" approach to getting media attention.):

http://tinyurl.com/qsh9ul

How to Plan Events with Social Media Tools:

http://mashable.com/2009/04/29/events-social-media/

How to Engage Mom Bloggers

http://tinyurl.com/ows429

Social Media Wiki (to see what other companies are doing on various social sites)

http://wiki.beingpeterkim.com/

Chapter 12: Using Social Media for an Online PR Campaign

Afterword

Now it's your turn to apply what you've learned. After your first press release, the cycle begins again. Once you market your online press release go and find a new topic. Create an editorial schedule (like a editorial schedule that magazines write up) so your marketing is continuous and consistent. For online PR campaigns, write a marketing plan using elements from this book. It can be very simple.

I welcome online PR success stories. Please go to http://www.OnlinePRBook.com and fill out the email form on the right hand side. Or, email me at janet@affiliateflash.com.

My hope is that you have learned enough to begin marketing your business online with online news as a foundation. However, if you need additional guidance, please contact me.

To your online success,

Janet Thaeler

Afterword

A Useful Blogs about Online Press Releases and PR

There are thousands of blogs about public relations. Here are a few you might want to add to your RSS reader (if you don't already have them).

TopRank Online Marketing Blog
http://tinyurl.com/npvv2a

A Shel of My Former Self
http://blog.holtz.com/

A View on PR from Silicon Valley
http://siliconvalleypr.blogspot.com/

Andy Lark's Blog
http://andylark.blogs.com/andylark/

Bad Pitch Blog
http://www.badpitch.blogspot.com/

Beyond the Hype
http://loispaul.typepad.com/

BlinnPR Report
http://blinnpr.com/blog/

D S Simon Vlog Views
http://www.dssimonvlogviews.com/

Digital PR Blog
http://www.prnewsonline.com/blog/

Einsight
http://www.scottpublicrelations.com/einsight/

Engage PR
http://blog.engagepr.com/

The Flack
http://theflack.blogspot.com

The Holmes Report Blog
http://holmesreport.com/blog/index.cfm

10e20
http://www.10e20.com/blog/

Ishmael's Corner
http://www.ishmaelscorner.com/

KDPaine's PR Measurement Blog
http://kdpaine.blogs.com/

Micro Persuasion
http://micropersuasion.com

PR 2.0
http://www.briansolis.com/index.htm

PR News Blog
http://www.prnewsonline.com/prnewsblog/

PR Squared
http://www.pr-squared.com/

Rich Edelman's 6 A.M.
http://edelman.com/speak_up/blog/

David Meerman Scott's blog
Author of the book 'The New Rules of Marketing and PR.'
http://www.webinknow.com

HARO blog
http://shankman.com

My Online PR & Social Media Blog
http://www.onlinePRBook.com

B Helpful Websites

http://www2.marketwire.com/mw/distribution_us lists US media outlets by state so you can visit their websites and find out who is covering the type of news you have. Find the small business editor, tech editor, or whoever is writing the topic and email them directly.

Huge list of international media contacts/journalists who are on Twitter, http://tinyurl.com/6wo3t2

Directory of people on Twitter searchable by topic, state, etc:
http://www.twellow.com

Another useful Twitter directory:
http://twitterholic.com identifies top twitter users by various categories.

Why Facebook: http://whyfacebook.com

Joan Stewart's The Publicity Hound:
http://bit.ly/Publicity: her newsletter, website and calls give you ideas on how to get publicity in old and new media. Her material is no nonsense and she gives plenty of practical advice and "how to."

The NewPR Wiki
http://www.thenewpr.com/wiki/pmwiki.php

Mashable: http://mashable.com

Here is a good source about creating buzz. Guy Kawasaki interviews Emanuel Rosen is the author of the national bestseller The Anatomy of Buzz (Doubleday, 2000) and The Anatomy of Buzz Revisited: Real-life lessons in Word-of-Mouth Marketing (Doubleday, 2009).

http://blogs.openforum.com/2009/02/11/the-art-of-generating-buzz/

http://tinyurl.com/qdpcsr

Media Post, http://www.mediapost.com - extensive directory to over 100,000 media, marketing and advertising professionals.

NewsLink.org, http://newslink.org - directory of newspapers and media outlets by state as well as the most linked to sites.

ABYZ News Links, http://www.abyznewslinks.com - directory for media contacts in different countries

C Online Press Release Distribution Sites

PR Newswire
(http://www.prnewswire.com/)
Page Rank 8/10
Traditional newswire. Must fill out membership application and pay $150 per year membership fee. Includes audio and video assistance, reports, editorial assistance, SEO assistance, etc.

EWorldWire.com
PageRank 5/10
Their "Major Newswire Distribution" domestic package goes to the Associated Pres, Reuters, MSNBC, CBS, ABC, etc. Cost is approximately $100. "Custom Online Newsroom with your logo, Basic Expert Copy Review, PDF, Archive (permanent), Focused & Targeted Categories (over 700), RSS feeds, (MSN, Google News, etc.), Clipping Report, and Translation." Many options for distribution including Top 100 Newspapers, College papers, radio talk show hosts, etc.—see http://tinyurl.com/mb7ymc.

Enhanced Online News ***BusinessWire associate
(http://eon.businesswire.com/)
Page Rank 7/10
$200 minimum optimized press release

PRWEb Direct
(http://www.prwebdirect.com/)
Page Rank 6/10
This is PRWeb's wire service—you can send your press release through the top two press release newswires like BusinessWire.

Free-Press-Release-Center.info
(http://www.freepressreleasecenter.com/)
Page Rank 6/10
Free but you can pay just a few dollars to get more features.
They are one of the few free press release sites that is well ranked, gets you into Google News, and offers keyword linking. The title of your press release becomes part of the URL—so if you use keywords in your title they will be in your URL. The only drawback is their URLs are so long that they are tough to manage and may be split (broken) when picked up by on other sites.

Internet News Bureau
(http://www.internetnewsbureau.com/)
Page Rank 6/10
$275/first submission - $80/subsequential submissions
Your press release is emailed to journalists as early as the next Business Day.

Click Press
(http://www.clickpress.com/)
Page Rank 6/10
I have had very good results using their $49 SEO press release.

Press box UK
(http://www.pressbox.co.uk/)
Page Rank 6/10
Free press release submission

Xpress Press News Service
(http://www.xpresspress.com/)
Page Rank 5/10
Starting prices $398
Leading provider of press releases via satellite

Press Kit 247
(http://www.presskit247.com/)
Page Rank 5/10
$99/mo
Press 24/7 puts you in control of your press kit and your press kit in front of the media. Gives you access to audio and video for your business.

UK Press Wire
(http://www.ukprwire.com/)
Page Rank 5/10
Free for UK & Global News Distribution.

US Press Wire
(http://www.usprwire.com/)
Page Rank 4/10
Free & $49
Appears to be another portal to Clickpress. URLs not optimized.

Advanced - PR
(http://www.advanced-pr.com/)
Page Rank 6/10
$249.00
Higher service PR site with many additional services.

Book Catcher
(http://www.bookcatcher.com/)
Page Rank 5/10
Free

BookCatcher.com (http://www.bookcatcher.com/) - for authors and book publishers with press releases and other resources.

Free-Press-Release
(http://free-press-release.com/)
Page Rank 5/10
Free and paying press releases
Only kept for 10 months but goes to Google News.

SB Wire
(http://sbwire.com/)
Page Rank 5/10
Prices as low as $19.95
Provides free press release distribution services for small to medium businesses. Can include company profile.

Send2Press
(http://www.send2press.com/)
Page Rank 5/10
Prices as low as $79.99
Another way to get targeted News Distribution and to major newswires.

PR Free
(http://www.prfree.com/)
Page Rank 5/10
Free

Rush PR News
(http://rushprnews.com/)
Page Rank 4/10
Prices starting at $35.00

PR Log
(http://tinyurl.com/lwaydm)
Page Rank 4/10
Free
PR Log offers free press release submission either immediately or scheduled date. Allows HTML and categorization of keywords.

URL Pitch
(http://urlpitch.com/)
Page Rank 4/10
No less than $50
Tell the world about your work

Press Method
(http://www.pressmethod.com/)
Page Rank 4/10
Free
Provides press release distribution, writing, and copy writing services.

ePress Release
(http://www.epressrelease.com/)
Page rank 4/10
Free
News release announcement services.

Online Press Releases
(http://onlinepressreleases.com/)
Page Rank 4/10
Free
Includes anchor text links and RSS feeds of your news.

The Open Press
(http://www.theopenpress.com/)
Page Rank 4/10
Free
Distributes media alerts and press releases to the mainstream media.
Free and commercial services available.

Fast Pitch! Press
(http://fastpitchpress.com/)
Page Rank 4/10
Free
Business Networking - press release distribution to the members of the
group no less than $14.95/mo

PR9.net
(http://www.pr9.net/)
Page Rank 4/10
Free
Basic and easy press release submission. Set up account and enter
your press release.

http://www.pressmethod.com
PageRank 4/10
Free
PressMethod provides feedback about the number of views your press
release receives.

Small Business Trends

If you're an entrepreneur or a small business you can submit your press release to this site free. You only get a link to one URL at the bottom but it has trust and can get visibility for your press release. http://smallbiztrends.com/category/press-release/

D Online Press Release Tips

Hubspot Press Release Grader

http://pressrelease.grader.com/ Run a press release through this grader and see how well it's optimized.

Online PR Checklist

Come up with a strong news story or angle—if possible tying the story into existing trends or hot topics.

Use keyword tools to do keyword research to determine three related keywords to focus on.

Collect related links, video, pictures, and graphics to illustrate your news.

Come up with a catchy title for a press release and/or use keywords in title.

Write the press release—I recommend it be about 300–500 words in length.

Determine what distribution service to use, upload your press release to service. Use keywords as links to relevant sections of website.

Write a blog post and link to the press release.

Bookmark the blog post on social bookmarking sites and ask others to.

Tweet about the news with a link to the blog post.

Identify key bloggers or members of the media that cover the subject of the news who might be interested in the news and email them the press release.

Promote the News:

Blog about the news on your blog with a keyword link back to the press release. Use a trackback to the press release if the service supports it.

Follow up with blog posts talking about any notable results—press coverage, blog coverage, or other outcomes you want to share.

Add your press release to your news page on your website with links intact (you can add additional links or pictures).

Ask other bloggers to write about the news and link to your post and the press release.

Email members of the media along with links to the post and the press release.

Write about your news release on your blog with a link to it on Twitter and have your employees retweet it (meaning that they share it with their Twitter network by putting the abbreviation RT before the message).

Bookmark the news and/or blog post on Delcious and have your employees and/or friends do it too. You can also pay someone to create additional bookmarks.

Submit your blog post to StumbleUpon and have your employees do the same.

Submit your news to Digg or Kirtsy and have your employees or others vote on it.

Submit your blog post to Faceboook and the press release (should have this set up to do automatically) and write about the results on your wall or to your Facebook Groups.

Create a Hubpage, Squidoo Page, or BundleIt page with more resources. Or, add to an existing page you've created if you have one that relates to the topic. You can bookmark these pages too.

Watch your web stats to see what is working and plan your future campaigns around that information. Look at your top referrers to your site. Recognize and reach out to those who have helped you and involve them in the future.

You can also reinforce your efforts with advertising—such as running paid search ads or paying for the sponsored section on StumbledUpon.

E Sample Email Pitches

Sample Pitch Email 1

{Greeting} {Name},

{Opening/ Introduction}

{Explanation of why your news is relevant to the person you're contacting—keep it brief as in bullet points}

{Tell them why this news might be important to them—remember to make this personable and relevant to what they write about}

{Link to the press release}

{Give you contact information and any additional information or links}

{Close},

{Your Name}

Sample Pitch Email 2

Hi _____,

I wanted to let you know that today we are excited to announce _____. The beta version is now available at _____.

Our product makes browsing the Internet more efficient by _____.

Our product lets you:

* Fill in forms with a single click

* Clip and collect content as you browse

* Get suggestions for broken links

Please let me know if you would like me to send a reviewers guide or if you have any questions.

Sincerely,

Sample Pitch Email 3

Hello _____,

I hope you are doing well. Please accept an advanced copy of our new book "_____."

I found your blog today and thought you and your readers would enjoy the book. It would be great if you could review the book for your blog readers and subscribers.

_____, the author, can provide any additional information that will add value to your blog and to your readers such as:

An interview

Answer Questions

Interview if you have a Blog Talk Radio or Teleconference

Giveaway of a book to your audience

Any follow up content or articles that will help your blog

Videos (describe topics)

The book is about (give a brief premise of the book's main points).

Please send me your mailing address if you are interested in reviewing the book so I can send you a complimentary copy. This is an advanced copy as the book is not yet in stores, but is scheduled to be released soon.

Please send the URL of the post when you review the book.

Thank You,

Name and Contact Info

Search Engine Marketing Glossary (excerpted from SEOBook.com)

Analytics

> Software which allows you to track your page views, user paths, and conversion statistics based upon interpreting your log files or through including a JavaScript tracking code on your site.

See also:

- **Google Analytics** - Google's free analytics program

- **Conversion Ruler** - a simple and cheap web based analytic tool

- **ClickTracks** - downloadable and web based analytics software

- **HitTail** - free and professional accounts at http://www.hittail.com

Anchor Text

> The text that a user would click on to follow a link. In the case the link is an image the image alt attribute may act in the place of anchor text.

Search engines assume that your page is authoritative for the words that people include in links pointing at your site. When links occur naturally they typically have a wide array of anchor text combinations. Too much similar anchor text may be a considered a sign of manipulation, and thus discounted or filtered. Make sure when you are building links that you control that you try to mix up your anchor text.

Example of anchor text:

<a href="http://www.seobook.com/">
Search Engine Optimization Blog</a>

Outside of your core brand terms if you are targeting Google you probably do not want any more than 10% to 20% of your anchor text to be the same. You can use Backlink Analyzer to compare the anchor text profile of other top ranked competing sites.

See also:

- **Backlink Analyzer** - free tool to analyze your link anchor text

Bookmarks

Most browsers come with the ability to bookmark your favorite pages. Many web based services have also been created to allow you to bookmark and share your favorite resources. The popularity of a document (as measured in terms of link equity, number of bookmarks, or usage data) is a signal for the quality of the information. Some search engines may eventually use bookmarks to help aid their search relevancy.

Social bookmarking sites are often called tagging sites. **Del.icio.us** is the most popular social bookmarking site.

See also:

- **Del.icio.us** - Yahoo! owned social bookmarking site

- **Yahoo! MyWeb** - similar to Del.icio.us, but more integrated into Yahoo!

- **Google Notebook** - allows you to note documents
- **Slashdot** - tech news site where stories are approved by central editors
- **Digg** - decentralized news site
- **Netscape** - Digg clone
- **Google Video** - Google's video hosting, tagging, and search site
- **YouTube** - popular decentralized video site

Brand

The emotional response associated with your company and/or products.

A brand is built through controlling customer expectations and the social interactions between customers. Building a brand is what allows you to move away from commodity based pricing and move toward higher margin value based pricing.

See also:

- **Rob Frankel** - branding expert who provides free branding question answers every Monday. He also offers *Frankel's Laws of Big Time Branding*™, blogs, and wrote the branding book titled 'The Revenge of Brand X. '

Branded Keywords

Keywords or keyword phrases associated with a brand. Typically branded keywords occur late in the buying cycle, and are some of the highest value and highest converting keywords.

CMS

Content Management System. Tool used to help make it easy to update and add information to a website. Blogs are a form of CMS that are typically SEO-friendly.

Comments

Many blogs and other content management systems allow readers to leave user feedback.

Leaving enlightening and thoughtful comments on someone else's related website is one way to help get them to notice you.

See also:

- **blog comment spam** - the addition of low value or no value comments to other's websites

Conversion

Many forms of online advertising are easy to track. A conversion is reached when a desired goal is completed.

Some marketers use custom phone numbers or coupon codes to tie offline activity to online marketing. You can measure conversion for a press release or on social media.

Here are a few common example desired goals

- a product sale

- completing a lead form

- a phone call

- capturing an email

- filling out a survey

- getting a person to pay attention to you

- getting feedback

- having a site visitor share your website with a friend

- having a site visitor link at your site

CTR

Clickthrough rate—the percentage of people who view click on an advertisement or press release they viewed, which is a way to measure how relevant a traffic source or keyword is. Search ads typically have a higher clickthrough rate than traditional banner ads due to being highly relevant to implied searcher demand.

To get the clickthrough rate for a press release, divide the number of "impressions" by the number of "reads."

Deep Link

A link which points to an internal page within a website.

When links grow naturally typically most high quality websites have many links pointing at interior pages. When you request links from other websites it makes sense to request a link from their most targeted relevant page to your most targeted relevant page. Some webmasters even create content based on easy linking opportunities they think up.

Domain

Scheme used for logical or location organization of the web. Many people also use the word domain to refer to a specific website.

External Link

Link which references another domain.

Linking to other related resources besides just your domain is a good way to help search engines understand what your site is about. If you link out to lots of low quality sites or primarily rely on low quality reciprocal links some search engines may not rank your site very well. Search engines are more likely to trust high quality editorial links (both to and from your site).

Headline

The title of an article or story.

Impression

Keyword

A word or phrase which implies a certain mindset or demand that targeted prospects are likely to search for.

Long tail and brand related keywords are typically worth more than shorter and vague keywords because they typically occur later in the buying cycle and are associated with a greater level of implied intent.

Keyword Density

An old measure of search engine relevancy based on how prominent keywords appeared within the content of a page. Keyword density is no longer a valid measure of relevancy over a broad open search index though.

If you use too many keywords in your press release or website copy it tends to read mechanically (and thus does not convert well and is not link worthy), plus some pages that are crafted with just the core keyword in mind often lack semantically related words and modifiers from the related vocabulary (and that causes the pages to rank poorly as well).

See also:

- The Keyword Density of Non Sense

- Keyword Density Analysis Tool

- Search Engine Friendly Copywriting—What Does 'Write Naturally' Mean for SEO?

Keyword Research

The process of discovering relevant keywords and keyword phrases to focus your SEO and PPC marketing campaigns on.

Example keyword discovery methods:

- using keyword research tools
- looking at analytics data or your server logs
- looking at page copy on competing sites
- reading customer feedback
- placing a search box on your site and seeing what people are looking for
- talking to customers to ask how and why they found and chose your business

Keyword Research Tools

Tools which help you discover potential keywords based on past search volumes, search trends, bid prices, and page content from related websites.

Short list of the most popular keyword research tools:

- **SEO Book Keyword Research Tool** - free, driven by Overture, this tool cross references all of my favorite keyword research tools. In addition to linking to traditional keyword research tools, it also links to tools such as Google Suggest, Buzz related tools, vertical databases, social bookmarking and tagging sites, and latent semantic indexing related tools.

- **Overture** - free, powered from Yahoo! search data. Heavily biased toward over representing commercial queries, combines singular and plural versions of a keyword into a single data point.

- **Google** - free tool that uses Google search data.

- **Wordtracker** - paid, powered from Dogpile and MetaCrawler. Due to small sample size their keyword database may be easy to spam.

- **Digital Point Keyword Suggestion Tool** - free keyword research tool which returns keyword research data from Overture and Wordtracker side by side.

Please note that most keyword research tools used alone are going to be highly inaccurate at giving exact quantitative search volumes. The tools are better for qualitative measurements. To test the exact volume for a keyword it may make sense to set up a test Google AdWords campaign.

Keyword Stuffing

Writing copy that uses excessive amounts of the core keyword.

When people use keyword stuffed copy it tends to read mechanically (and thus does not convert well and is not link worthy), plus some pages that are crafted with just the core keyword in mind often lack semantically related words and modifiers from the related vocabulary (and that causes the pages to rank poorly as well).

See also:

- Search Engine Friendly Copywriting—What Does 'Write Naturally' Mean for SEO?

Organic Search Results

Most major search engines have results that consist of paid ads and unpaid listings. The unpaid/algorithmic listings are called the organic search results. Organic search results are organized by relevancy, which is largely determined based on linkage data, page content, usage data, and historical domain and trust related data.

Most clicks on search results are on the organic search results. Some studies have shown that 60 to 80% + of clicks are on the organic search results.

ROI

Return on Investment is a measure of how much return you receive from each marketing dollar.

While ROI is a somewhat sophisticated measurement, some search marketers prefer to account for their marketing using more sophisticate profit elasticity calculations.

RSS

Rich Site Summary or **Real Simple Syndication** is a method of syndicating information to a feed reader or other software which allows people to subscribe to a channel they are interested in.

Search Engine

A tool or device used to find relevant information on the Internet. Search engines consist of a spider, index, relevancy algorithms and search results.

SEO

Search engine optimization is the art and science of publishing information and marketing it in a manner that helps search engines understand your information is relevant to relevant search queries.

SEO consists largely of keyword research, SEO copywriting, information architecture, link building, brand building, building mindshare, reputation management, and viral marketing.

SEO Title

Writing and formatting copy in a way that will help make your press release appear relevant to a wide array of relevant search queries.

There are two main ways to write titles and be SEO friendly

1. Write literal titles that are well aligned with things people search for. This works well if you need backfill content for your site or already have an amazingly authoritative site.
2. Write page titles that are exceptionally compelling to link to. If enough people link at them then your pages and site will rank for many relevant queries even if the keywords are not in the page titles.

Social Media

Websites which allow users to create the content. A few examples of social media sites are social bookmarking sites and social news sites and communities. Twitter, Facebook, and LinkedIn are examples of social media sites.

Technorati

Blog search engine which tracks popular stories and link relationships.

See also:

• Technorati.com

URL

Uniform Resource Locator is the unique address of any web document.

Wordpress

Popular open source blogging software platform, offering both a downloadable blogging program and a hosted solution.

If you are serious about building a brand or making money online you should publish your content to your own domain because it can be hard to reclaim a website's link equity and age related trust if you have built years of link equity into a subdomain on someone else's website.

See also:

- **Wordpress.org** - download the software

- **Wordpress.com** - offers free blog hosting

About the Author

Janet began her career at Internet startup companies as a web developer until she determined her true passion is marketing—specifically Internet marketing. She is a professional writer and blogger whose work has been published in both offline and online magazines including *City Search*. She has presented to business owners and the PRSSA.

Janet has been employed as a business-to-business tech marketer, a web-marketing manager, and a brand managing and strategy coordinator. In addition to her own consulting, she writes SEO press releases and specializes in Social Media at OrangeSoda.

As a coach she has helped many businesses of all sizes start blogs and learn about social media and online PR tools. She is not only an evangelist of social media but she is actively involved, beginning as a blogger in 2005.

She blogs on Marketing Pilgrim (http://www.marketingpilgrim.com) and is a guest blogger at Small Business Trends (http://www.smallbiztrends.com/blog). Her blog can be found at www.newspapergrl.com Follow her on Twitter at http://www.twitter.com/newspapergrl.

Other Happy About® Books

Purchase these books at Happy About
http://happyabout.info
or at other online and physical bookstores.

JASON ALBA
Foreword by Bob Burg

I'm on LinkedIn—Now What???

This book explains the benefits of using LinkedIn and recommendsbest practices so that you can getthe most out of it.

Paperback $19.95
eBook $14.95

JASON ALBA & JESSE STAY
Foreword by Lee Lorenzen   Afterword by Robert Scoble

I'm on Facebook—Now What???

This book will help you come up with your own action strategy to get value out of Facebook.

Paperback $19.95
eBook $14.95

42 Rules of Marketing

Compilation of ideas, theories, and practical approaches to marketing challenges that marketers know they should do, but don't always have the time or patience to do.

Paperback $19.95
eBook $11.95

Twitter Means Business

For companies unfamiliar with Twitter, this book serves as a field guide. They will get a Twitterverse tour, and learn about the dozens of firms big and small that have harnessed Twitter as a powerful, flexible business tool.

Paperback $19.95
eBook $14.95

9 781600 051548